PALS
7.80

D0643838

*Local Notables and the City Council*

# Local Notables
# and the City Council

ROGER V. CLEMENTS

*Macmillan*

*First published 1969 by*
MACMILLAN AND CO LTD
*Little Essex Street London* WC2
*and also at Bombay Calcutta and Madras*
*Macmillan South Africa (Publishers) Pty Ltd Johannesburg*
*The Macmillan Company of Australia Pty Ltd Melbourne*
*The Macmillan Company of Canada Ltd Toronto*
*Gill and Macmillan Ltd Dublin*

*Printed in Great Britain by*
R. & R. CLARK LTD
*Edinburgh*

*to*
*Matthew,*
*Virginia*
*and Rosemary*

# Contents

# List of Tables

A 2

CHAPTER 1

# Introduction

POLITICAL participation in its manifold variety is an aspect of behaviour which has received a good deal of attention from political scientists since the war. Statistical studies and attitude-surveys have widened our knowledge of electoral behaviour; interpretations in psychological terms of people's relations to the political system have deepened our understanding of what politics can mean to the individual citizen; cross-cultural comparison of the extent and types of political participation and of attitudes towards it has been yet another rewarding approach to the problem. A great deal of progress has been made in adding to our knowledge of the varieties of political men and something of the personal, social and cultural influences which help to form their roles in the political system. We have a long way to go, however, before we can predict with certainty (if we ever can) the political actions and inaction of any given individual; and we are still ignorant of many details of, and the reasons for, the patterns of participation by particular groups. If answers to questions about them are required we still have to undertake specific empirical investigations in order to provide them.

The present study centres upon an attempt to solve just such a problem concerning the particular pattern of political participation by a specific group of people,

Why do notables otherwise active in society not seek to take part, as members, in the work of their local councils? What does the sort of pattern of activity and what do the roles that can accommodate such behaviour look like, and can their characteristics be explained? These questions in their turn arose out of the very practical current concern about the 'quality' of councillors.

Like anxiety about the 'quality' of M.P.s, this concern has a long history. Corruption was perhaps regarded as the special besetting sin of early nineteenth century local councillors but allegations also of incompetence were not uncommon. At one point in its critical report on Bristol, the 1835 Royal Commission on Municipal Corporations solemnly stated, 'we think the Corporation stands entirely clear of any imputation of clandestinely appropriating its public revenues to individual profit, but it cannot be so easily acquitted of mismanagement and extravagance'.[1] It is upon their alleged incompetence that most modern strictures now turn.

Though serious attempts to define what is meant by 'quality' in councillors have been highly exiguous,[2] the argument is often explicitly or implicitly in terms of 'administrative' or 'managerial' ability, though these are

[1] Royal Commission on Municipal Corporations (1835), Appendix to 1st Report, para. II, p. 1222.

[2] For some discussion see A. M. Rees and T. Smith, *Town Councillors: a Study of Barking* (The Acton Society Trust, 1964) pp. 95–109; also the report of the committee on the management of local government, *Management of Local Government* (The 'Maud Report'), 5 vols (H.M.S.O., 1967) vol I, *Report of the Committee*, pp. 142–4; and F. Bealey, J. Blondel and W. P. McCann, *Constituency Politics* (Faber, 1965) p. 409. The best discussion of the problem is probably in L. J. Sharpe, 'Elected Representatives in Local Government', in *British Journal of Sociology*, XIII (1962) 201–4; but it does not pretend to be exhaustive.

hardly more exact expressions. It is said that there is a deficiency of administrative ability in local councils because men endowed with it find local government service unattractive. Critics have seen in this failing an important, or even the most serious, weakness in the local government system. John Stuart Mill wrote in 1861, 'the greatest imperfection of popular local institutions, and the chief cause of the failure which so often attends them, is the low calibre of the men by whom they are almost always carried on'.[1]

This mediocre assessment of councillors has indeed long been a widespread vulgar commonplace, as jokes, television portrayals and newspaper comment abundantly testify, and it appears to be accepted by many councillors themselves. A study of Barking town councillors showed that most had reservations about the quality of candidates and even councillors, and my own inquiries have elicited similar modest assessments of their candidates by party officials in Bristol.[2] The Maud Report tells us that the recruitment of adequate people is felt to be a problem in almost all the authorities visited.[3] The difficulty and importance of manning councils with able men and women has long been part of the central government's official conventional wisdom; the war-time white paper, *Local Government in England and Wales during the period of Reconstruction*, regarded the task confronting the administration as one of strengthening the local government framework to bear greater responsibilities and new tasks, but, it went on, 'the solution of the problem turns largely on the

[1] J. S. Mill, *Representative Government* (World's Classics ed., 1912) pp. 369–70.
[2] Rees and Smith, *Town Councillors*, pp. 96–8. See also A. H. Birch, *Small-Town Politics: Glossop* (O.U.P., 1959) p. 115.
[3] Maud Report, I 474.

capacity and public spirit of the persons who, as members and officers of the local authorities, are prepared to devote their services to local authorities'.[1]

There has also come to be agreement upon two propositions – that such competent people might be recruited to local government from the professional, business, middle and upper classes,[2] and that too few of our local representatives do at present come from these sources. Dame Evelyn Sharp, as Permanent Secretary to the Ministry of Housing and Local Government, gave a striking address on 'the Future of Local Government' to an audience in Bristol in 1962, saying, *inter alia*, 'I do not think that enough really able people are interested today in taking part in local government. I do not think enough people from business, from industry, from agriculture, from the professions are going into it . . . of course, there are some very able people in the business; but there aren't enough, and not enough good recruits are coming forward.'[3] Similarly, the Lord Mayor of Bristol has appealed to local industry, commerce and the banks 'to allow some of your best brains to come forward to seek election to the Council'.[4] However, Mill had already noticed that local office was not 'in general sought by the higher ranks',[5]

[1] H.M.S.O. (1945) Cmd 6579, p. 2.

[2] At one stage the Maud Report uses membership of these groups as a possible yardstick of high calibre, but it goes on to point out that such people occupy a disproportionately large number of seats on councils, and that the qualities the Report finally identifies as desirable 'can be discovered in all levels of society' (Maud Report, I 142–3). One suspects that the make-up of a Royal Commission, an advisory body or a Regional Hospital Board is often the model.

[3] *Municipal Review*, Aug 1962, p. 516.

[4] (Bristol) *Evening Post*, 8 Feb 1967.

[5] Mill, *Representative Government*, p. 365. Indeed, 'the local representative bodies and their officers are almost certain to be

and the rather remote case of Lord Rosebery suggests the long-established character of the apparent rule that on the whole the business and professional 'notables', and the middle and upper classes, have not been persuaded to serve in local government to the extent that their accepted position in our society has led many to expect.[1]

It was within this climate of opinion that the Maud Committee was established in 1963 by the Minister on the suggestion of the local-authority associations to investigate problems relating to the managerial efficiency of councils and their members. In accomplishing part of this task the Committee used the resources of the Government Social Survey to interview a national sample of electors on its attitudes to local government, and more intensive studies were also made of councillors and ex-councillors. Among topics put forward or considered at a meeting at Nuffield College in the summer of 1964, when the Maud Committee was commencing its inquiries, was the problem of explaining why people who are influential, prominent and active in various forms of voluntary work do not join their local Council. On the face of it, leadership in the formal local political

---

of a much lower grade of intelligence and knowledge than Parliament and the national executive' (ibid. p. 375).

[1] 'Where is the latter day Rosebery to chair the new Greater London Council as he did the nascent London County Council?' (L. J. Sharpe, *Why Local Democracy* (Fabian Tract 361, (1965) p. 1.) For their desertion of their local councils by leading businessmen, and the growth of divisions between the social, economic and political leadership in Cheshire, Glossop, Newcastle under Lyme and South Wales, see J. M. Lee, *Social Leaders and Public Persons* (O.U.P. 1963) p. 55; Birch, *Small-Town Politics*, pp. 115, 131; Bealey, *et al.*, *Constituency Politics*, pp. 25–8, 399, 409, 411; T. Brennan, E. W. Cooney and H. Pollins, *Social Change in South-West Wales* (Watts, 1954) p. 177.

system could well be expected to be a 'natural'[1] and necessary part of the social role of such notables in the community – more so than that of any other group – and the question inevitably arises why then do they not adopt it – why are the economic and social notables not also political notables? These are also the people from among whom, as we have seen, it is widely thought more competent councillors might and should be recruited.

Though there has been little investigation into this problem, there seems to be a large measure of agreement on the probable solutions. A 'streamlining' of the internal organisation of the Council, including a reduction in the number and work of committees, is often proposed – for example, by the Lord Mayor of Bristol, and also by the report of the Maud Committee.[2] Some credence is given to another theory, that party politics or identification with a particular party is so obnoxious to these people as to prevent their participation, but it tends to be played down as an important factor, for instance by Dame Evelyn Sharp.[3] Mr J. G. Bulpitt, also, in his study of politics in local government, comes to the general conclusion that 'dominance of the municipal elections by the national parties as such did not appear

[1] Some writers use this expression apparently without reflecting upon its implications; Lee refers to the upper social classes of Cheshire as its 'natural' social leaders, and suggests that those of them killed in the First World War 'should' have provided the leaders of the 1930s (*Social Leaders*, pp. 92, 103). Similarly Bealey, Blondel and McCann speak of Newcastle under Lyme being deprived of its 'natural' leadership owing to its lack of industry (*Constituency Politics*, p. 38). The persistence of deferential attitudes is discussed in R. Rose, *Politics in England* (Faber, 1965) pp. 40–2.

[2] (Bristol) *Evening Post*, 8 Feb 1967; Maud Report I 63, 145.

[3] Also Rees and Smith, *Town Councillors*, p. 104; and Maud Report, I 115, 392.

to restrict the field of possible candidates for Council . . . candidates seemed far more influenced by business commitments, the time of council meetings and the eventual work-load than by the prospect of having to fight what would be, in most cases, a rather tepid party contest'.[1]

Another remedy for this dilemma, sometimes advanced, is an enlargement of either or both the areas and powers of local corporations to make them sufficiently important arenas of activity to attract energetic, able, high-status people. As Dame Evelyn put it, 'part of the trouble in getting good enough people to serve arises I believe from the fact that the areas and status of local authorities are often today too cramped or too small to enable a satisfactory job to be done'.[2] Testimony in favour of this point of view may be found in a variety of sources.[3] H. G. Wells argued strongly – before 1903 – that only 'better' (implying bigger) administrative areas would draw the 'ex-urban' classes – the wealthy, the lively, the educated, the intelligent – to participate in local affairs; he attacked the point of view represented by Belloc who 'dreams of a beautiful little village community of peasant proprietors, each sticking like a barnacle to his own little bit of property, beautifully healthy and simple and illiterate and Roman Catholic

[1] J. G. Bulpitt, *Party Politics in English Local Government* (Longmans, 1967) p. 96.

[2] *Municipal Review*, p. 519. Also the Maud Report, I 84: 'The freedoms we advocate for local authorities, together with increased financial autonomy and more powerful local authority units, would, we believe, do much to attract people of calibre to the service of local authorities. . . .'

[3] J. S. Mill wrote (in support of 'most purpose' authorities), 'Now it is quite hopeless to induce persons of a high class, either socially or intellectually, to take a share of local administration in a corner by piecemeal, as members of a Paving Board or a Drainage Commission' (*Representative Government*, p. 370).

and *local*, local over the ears. I am afraid the stars in their courses fight against such pink and golden dreams.'[1] Like many others, Wells preferred to side with the stars in their courses. The pioneering report of the Barlow Commission on the *Distribution of the Industrial Population* showed the Commission to be exercised by the administrative obstacles placed by the traditional pattern and functioning of local government in the way of any proposals requiring the planned use of land and economic resources. *Inter alia* they said, 'some evidence was given that the calibre of those who administer the larger units of local government today is tending to decline. Councils and committees to be manned are numerous, alike in county and borough; the work is arduous, and volunteers of good administrative ability are not always easy to find. The establishment of councils, few in number and with considerable powers over wide regional areas would, it is anticipated, tend to attract those possessing a high standard of administrative ability, both in town and country life. . . .'[2] Recently the evidence of the Ministry of Housing and Local Government to the Royal Commission on Local Government has argued the same point.[3]

I therefore undertook an investigation among active notables in Bristol, a city of some 430,000 inhabitants, to try to find out why they avoid membership of the county borough Council.[4] In so far as their presence

---

[1] A paper on administrative areas, read before the Fabian Society, reprinted in *Area and Power*, ed. A. Maas (Free Press of Glencoe, Chicago, 1959) pp. 214–15.

[2] H.M.S.O. (1940) Cmd 6153, p. 182.

[3] Royal Commission on Local Government in England. Written evidence of the Ministry of Housing and Local Government (H.M.S.O., 1967) p. 73.

[4] I am indebted to Mr Louis Moss of the Government Social Survey for showing me the questions being put to the electorate

on local councils is considered desirable, conceivably successful action might then follow to encourage it. Moreover, such persons, with experience in a variety of comparable spheres, might also be expected to offer useful diagnoses of the ills afflicting local government with a wider application. Besides, since they are by definition 'influential', presumably they have a disproportionate effect on general opinion, and therefore their views on local authorities (as on other topics) have special weight in popular assessments of council work, and therefore have added significance. But it was also recognised that it might not be sufficient to seek answers merely at the level of revealing practical obstacles in the way of council service, with consequential recommendations for their removal; but that some attention should also be paid to the local community structure, to the role of these people in, and their attitudes to, the political system, and to the ensuing pattern of their political behaviour. The views of local notables about representative democracy and so forth are of some importance in assessing their actual and potential role in local government – for example, do they value representative government as providing scope for wide participation and the extensive sharing of responsibilities, or are 'experts' (elected or appointed) preferred to 'ordinary' people in power? Is their usual 'style' of decision-making and responsibility-bearing compatible with the usual assumptions of a representative system based on a universal franchise? Do their views of their role and of their interests in the community set limits to the degree of their participation in the political process?

---

and councillors on behalf of the Maud Committee. This helped me to formulate my own. I am also obliged to Mr Moss for initiating the discussion which led to this study.

Some light has been shed on these problems by a number of recent valuable studies of local political systems, of parties and local elections, of pressure groups (little at local level), of local communities and of political participation in general. Subjects for comment in these and other contexts include different kinds and degrees of political participation, of kinds and degrees of political indifference and ignorance. But the focal points, the major matters of study, tend to be separate kinds of participation, whether voting, party membership, political leadership and so forth, not the over-all style of political participation by particular groups of people. Thus, while attention has been paid to the changing kinds of political leadership forthcoming at different times, there is a tendency to lose interest in a group once it has been shown no longer to play a leading part in political life, and interest transfers to the current actors at the forefront of the stage.[1] In particular, no extended probing has been attempted, so far as I am aware, of reasons why contemporary, active and powerful social and economic leaders in a community are not also its political leaders, nor of what, then, is the part played by local notables in municipal government. In essence this is what the present study seeks to do.

Bristol was chosen, not because it is a 'typical' city or community, but because I live there. Indeed, Bristol has interesting peculiarities in its history and in its political, social and economic development, not all of which have been thoroughly explored. It is relevant to this study that A. H. Birch, H. V. Wiseman, and J. G. Bulpitt, as well as the second volume of the Maud Report, have convincingly demonstrated the variety of political

[1] Rose points out that there has been no explanation for the failure to seek a leadership role by many of those early socialised to undertake one (*Politics in England*, p. 107n.).

systems in English local government.[1] Unlike some
other large towns, local politics in Bristol have been
firmly organised, indeed, almost monopolised, by the
Labour and Conservative (or Citizen)[2] parties for the
past few decades, and according to the Bulpitt typology[3]
may be classified as a mature two-party system. The
Labour and Citizen parties alternate in power, and in
over forty years only between 1959 and 1963 have there
been councillors who were neither Citizen nor Labour
in allegiance. This necessarily to some extent colours
the attitudes of local notables to service on the local
Council – as we shall see some express themselves more
sympathetically towards 'independent' rural politics.
We can be sure that not everything that is true about the
political participation of the notables in Bristol will be
true of the participation of notables elsewhere.

And yet some of the major peculiarities of Bristol are
ones of moderation: its growth and prominence have
been remarkably continuous over several centuries;[4] its
economy is highly diversified; it has long been a seaport
as well as a manufacturing and important commercial
centre; its industries are most varied, and it has a few

[1] Birch, *Small-Town Politics*, passim; Bulpitt, *Party Politics*,
passim; H. V. Wiseman, 'Local Government in Leeds', in *Public
Administration*, XLI (1963) 51, 137; Maud Report, vol. II, *The
Local Government Councillor*, passim.

[2] The group on the Council is called the Citizen Party. It ori-
ginated in the early 1920s from an anti-Socialist pact between the
Liberals and Conservatives, who formerly jointly dominated
Bristol, but the links with the Conservative Party are now so
close and singular, and so similar to those in other cities between
Conservative council groups and the Conservative Party, that it
would be misleading to attach significance to the difference in
nomenclature.

[3] Bulpitt, *Party Politics*, pp. 123–30.

[4] See W. G. Hoskins, *Local History in England* (Longmans,
1959); app. 'The Ranking of Provincial Towns 1334–1861', pp.
174–8.

large firms as well as many smaller ones; its prosperity has been steady and it has always avoided the lowest depths of depression; though possessing a large rural hinterland and a life independent of the metropolis it has not been isolated from London and the forces of modern industrialism; the proportions of social and occupational groups amongst its inhabitants are remarkably near the average for the urbanised parts of the country; it has its slums, its housing and welfare problems, but these again are manageable compared with other cities. In a close statistical study of 157 British towns utilising sixty variables, it was found that Bristol appeared least frequently in extreme positions in the various series.[1] These facts, together with such general arguments as the relative homogeneity of this country and the centralised character of its political and administrative systems, as well as the presence in all our large cities of similar problems of planning, housing, traffic, education and so on, make it not altogether absurd to suggest that at least the broad outlines of the discussion about the relations between the notables and the local authority in Bristol may be applicable to conditions in other large towns.[2]

Nor was the choice of the sample of economic and social notables for interview made by 'scientific' methods. The following criteria of selection were employed. Firstly, the members of the sample should

[1] C. A. Moser and W. Scott, *British Towns* (Oliver & Boyd, 1961) p. 39. Compare the rank-orders of Bristol in the various series (pp. 120, 121) with those of similar-sized towns.

[2] The long, slow evolution of Bristol's social system in association with the steady development of its economy may well, however, be a crucial distinction in comparison with towns experiencing more dramatic economic changes. Cf. Margaret Stacey, *Tradition and Change: A Study of Banbury* (O.U.P., 1960) pp. 11–19.

not currently be local councillors, and if they had
formerly been councillors they were not to be included
had they given up merely through ill-health, defeat or
old age. This criterion therefore excludes the town's
political notables. Secondly, they should have been
active in voluntary community work, whether professional, business, charitable, welfare or connected with
public bodies. Thirdly, they should be considered to
have some influence and prominence by such people as
the Bishop, the Vice-Chancellor, the Secretary of the
Trades Council or the President of the Chamber of
Commerce, who, among others, were asked to supply
names.[1] A few more were nominated by people I interviewed. It was felt that to list organisations and interview
their officers would beg the question as to their position
in the larger society; it would have excluded the (re-
putedly) richest businessman in the city as he has hitherto
belonged almost solely to those bodies set up by himself.

In view of the controversy that has raged in America
between proponents (such as Floyd Hunter and D. C.
Miller[2]) of the 'reputational' technique for identifying
community notables, and, on the other hand, supporters
(like Dahl, Polsby or Wildavsky[3]) of the study of

[1] I also invited the leaders of the two parties on the Council to
assist the research by suggesting names: the leader of the Citizen
Party felt he could not properly assist; the leader of the Labour
Party, with which I associated until Feb 1968, did not reply.

[2] F. Hunter, *Community Power Structure* (University of North
Carolina Press, Chapel Hill, 1953); D. C. Miller, 'Decision-
Making Cliques in Community Power Structures', in *American
Journal of Sociology*, LXIV (Nov 1958) 299–310. Miller compares
Seattle and Bristol. For an English exercise in this *genre*, see
Birch, *Small-Town Politics*, pp. 41–3.

[3] R. A. Dahl, *Who Governs?* (Yale U.P., New Haven, Conn.,
1961); N. Polsby, *Community Power and Political Theory* (Yale
U.P., New Haven, Conn., 1963); A. Wildavsky, *Leadership in a
Small Town* (Bedminster Press, Totowa, N.J., 1964).

decision-making to identify leaders, it should perhaps be emphasised that the present study did not set out to discover the 'real' leaders of Bristol. It sought to discover why a sample of people 'one might expect' to participate as representatives in local government do not do so. It was assumed that these expectations might legitimately be aroused because, first, there was evidence of heavy commitments by these people to voluntary activities of other sorts, suggesting energy, public spirit, interest and some liking for public work, and, second, because the people concerned were sufficiently accustomed to being in the public eye and possessed of a reputation for getting things done for their absence from the Council to be regarded as something of a puzzle. To build up the sample partly on the basis of having some reputation for possessing 'influence' was therefore not an attempt to pin down and grade *the* leaders of the community but merely to identify *some* of those whose position and activity in society are, on the face of it, analogous to those of the political leadership to which, however, they refuse to be recruited.

Invitations to be interviewed were extended to some ninety of the list of roughly one hundred and thirty names, of whom seventy-nine were interviewed, but as one failed to meet my criteria, evidence from seventy-eight people only is utilised here. Only one or two outright refusals were encountered; a few were absent when approached. Interviews on the average took one and a quarter hours; sometimes under one hour, sometimes over two hours. They took place in 1965 and 1966.[1]

Members of the sample were selected according to

[1] I should like to record my deep gratitude to members of the sample for their kindness in giving up their time to me and for the patience with which they answered my questions. I hope they will feel at least that the result is enlightening.

spread of occupation, the frequency with which they were mentioned and also according to my general knowledge about their position in the business, professional and social life of the city. Amongst them are leaders in the legal, medical and accountancy professions; prominent clergymen of several denominations; highly placed educators; top managers and directors of large retail stores, chains of retail shops, stockbroking firms, building societies, banks and estate agents; leading proprietors, chairmen or directors of large aeroplane, shoe-manufacturing, wine-importing, tobacco, brewing, packaging, chocolate, newspaper, shipping and building firms; members of smaller engineering, chemical, milling, contracting and fine-art companies, as well as a large public utility; two leading trade union officials; and women active in voluntary organisations and public work.

The terms 'prominent' or 'influential' do not provide a very objective standard, but the method of selection appears to have produced a group who do, directly and indirectly, in the long and the short term, considerably affect decisions impinging upon the lives of many people in this city in quite important and diverse ways. Only the evidence of the jobs and economic positions they fill can be offered as evidence for this assertion here; but even the most pluralistic of theorists would accept that these people have a disproportionately large share of influence.[1] Amongst them are high social status – even if deference is not what it was; much economic power – however hedged about by trade unions, government, the market and limiting conventions; and a concentration of rare technical and professional skills. It is not claimed

---

[1] That resources for influence are often most unequally distributed and utilised is accepted and indeed demonstrated by Dahl, Polsby, Banfield, Wildavsky and others.

that these seventy-eight are the seventy-eight most influential people in the city. They do not all have the same standing, for the degree of influence wielded by individual members of the group varies widely, and certainly of a few it could be said that there are hundreds of people in the city who could as well qualify to be included. But nobody living here, seeing the list of names, would dispute that amongst them are thirty or forty of the most influential personages in Bristol.[1] They include members of the peerage, knights,[2] scions of old aristocratic families, and at least two millionaires; men and women who have the entrée to Whitehall's corridors, who sit on, or preside over, committees of inquiry and advisory bodies and central committees of voluntary groups; some who are internationally known, others who have been phenomenal post-war business successes, and yet others who have maintained a more modest but lengthy family tradition of business or professional enterprise, combined with service in honorific posts like sheriff, or deputy lieutenant of the county, and so forth.[3]

[1] Even Wildavsky admits that informants mentioned as influential half those whom he 'proved' to be 'leaders' in his decisional case-studies (*Leadership*, p. 312). It would be an odd democracy where the proportion were lower. Whitehall, too, would be surprised, even chagrined, if some, at least, of the sample were not 'influential' in Bristol – and elsewhere. Several were identified as 'influentials' by Miller, in *American Journal of Sociology*, LXIV 309.

[2] One was knighted later. Fourteen of the sample are listed in *Who's Who*, and several others have close relatives included there.

[3] Subsequent to the interview stage the 'Harlech Consortium' was set up to bid for the commercial television franchise in Wales and the West. Of the twenty-three members, eight are based in Bristol; of these eight, six had been included in the sample. On criteria which, according to *The Times* (13 June 1967), consisted of a 'sort of establishment rating put on their names' this syndicate successfully ousted the incumbent T.W.W.

Their suitability according to the other criteria – their absence from the Council, and their activity in voluntary affairs – is easily established. There is no reason to believe, therefore, that the sample is not highly representative of the sort of people in whose views I was interested.

## POSTSCRIPT

With the recent deaths of Sir Egbert Cadbury and Mr A. W. Bryant, there seems to be no reason to conceal the fact that they were members of the sample, especially as none of their remarks has been directly or indirectly quoted in this work. Some aspects of their lives and careers will shed light on the nature of the sample.

Born in Birmingham in 1893, the younger son of George Cadbury, the founder of Bourneville, Sir Egbert Cadbury attended first, Leighton Park School (a Friends school) at Reading, then Trinity College, Cambridge. In the First World War he saw service in the Navy and Air Force, then came to Bristol in 1919 to join J. S. Fry & Sons, making his permanent home here. In 1920 he became managing director; and from 1943 till his retirement in 1963 he was also managing director of Cadbury Brothers Ltd. Other firms of which he was a director included Lloyds Bank, Keith Prowse, and Daily News Ltd, and he was chairman of Willetts Investments Ltd. His public positions included that of Regional Controller of the South-Western Region for the Minister of Fuel and Power from 1941 to 1950, and he was also chairman of the Central Transport Consultative Committee from 1948 to 1954, sitting in London. A J.P. since 1928, for a long time he was chairman of the local petty sessions in the rural district in which he lived bordering Bristol, the centre of which is about three miles (across Brunel's suspension bridge) from his residence. Sir Egbert Cadbury's positions within the voluntary social service field included the treasurership of the Bristol Royal Infirmary from 1922; he was also connected with the United Bristol Hospitals after 1948. Besides being a Vice-President of the executive committee of the National Association of Boys' Clubs, he was chairman for twenty years of the Bristol Federation of Boys' Clubs. He was a member and had served his year as Master of the Merchant Venturers Society, and was connected with local charitable societies like the Grateful and the Dolphin. Till he retired at sixty-five he was a member of the Gloucestershire division of the Territorial Association; and as a member of the British Legion was president of 'one or two' branches. He enjoyed riding, shooting, golf and yachting, and he belonged to the Royal Thames Yacht Club amongst others. Besides all this he was president of the committee of the Bristol Citizen organisation which collects money for the Citizen Party (that is, the Conservative Party on Bristol Council). When Sir Egbert Cadbury died he left £1,300,000.

It will perhaps further illuminate the character of my sample if I suggest that, by a very rough estimate, Sir Egbert came within the top twenty in terms of over-all economic, social and political significance in the Bristol area, but he was outside the top five.

Mr A. W. Bryant, who died in June 1967 at the age of seventy-five, belonged to an old Bristol family. Since Joseph Bryant became a freeman of the city in 1718 there has always been a Bryant on the freemen's roll, and Mr A. W. Bryant was so honoured in 1912. He was also the seventh generation of his family to control the cordage- and canvas-manufacturing business which he entered on leaving his grammar school at the age of fifteen.

He felt his whole life to be bound up with Bristol, within whose borders he lived, and, in the words of his obituary, 'a defender of old Bristol customs and traditions, he found errors in the status of the city galling'.[1] As president of the Bristol Civic Society, he played a prominent part in preserving some of the city's notable buildings. He was a member of the Bristol Club from 1921, and he became secretary in 1947 and president in 1955 of the Anchor (charitable) Society. Similarly, after joining Rotary in 1920 Mr Bryant was elected successively secretary and president locally, and also chairman of the Rotary District Council. He played a large part in the foundation of the Bristol Council of Social Service, and became chairman of its finance committee. He was, besides, prominent locally in the Boy Scouts movement. In 1946 Mr Bryant was appointed to the magistrates' bench, and he was chosen to be Sheriff of Bristol in 1956.

[1] (Bristol) *Evening Post*, 8 June 1967.

# CHAPTER 2

# Some Characteristics of the Sample

AMONG those originally consulted as to the kind of person who conformed to the criteria of selection there was near unanimity; indeed, there was very often agreement on particular individuals. Members of the resultant sample belong overwhelmingly to what is popularly called the middle class. The following table shows the present distribution of the sample amongst 'socio-economic' groups as defined by the Registrar-General. Women without paid occupation are deemed to enjoy their husband's status.

A crude attempt to classify them in terms of social-

TABLE 1    Socio-economic groups[1]

|  | No. | % |
|---|---|---|
| 1. Employers or managers in large establishments | 49 | 62·8 |
| 2. Employers or managers in small establishments | 0 | 0 |
| 3. Professionals – self-employed | 15 | 19·2 |
| 4. Professionals – employees | 12 | 15·4 |
| 5. Intermediate non-manual (non-degree) | 2 | 2·6 |
| 6–17. All others | 0 | 0 |
| Total | 78 | 100 |

[1] See Registrar-General, *Classification of Occupations* (H.M.S.O., 1966).

class origin, utilising information about family background, education and father's occupation gives the results displayed below in Table 2. A similar analysis of the members of 'old Bristol families' – that is, families prominent in the city for at least two generations – in the sample is also incorporated in the table.

TABLE 2    Social-class origins

|  | Whole sample | | Bristol family | |
|---|---|---|---|---|
|  | No. | % | No. | % |
| 1. Working class | 4 | 5 | 0 | 0 |
| 2. Lower-middle class | 16 | 21 | 2 | 5 |
| 3. Middle class | 26 | 33 | 13 | 33 |
| 4. Upper-middle class | 24 | 31 | 16 | 41 |
| 5. Upper class | 8 | 10 | 8 | 21 |
| 6. Total | 78 | 100 | 39 | 100 |

Table 2 does not have the same objective value as Table 1, and no stress can be laid in particular on the divisions within the middle class. In so far as the sample is an accurate one, it underlines the difficulty encountered by working-class people in joining those considered 'influential', except by way of powerful working-class organisations, and that most rarely. Two of the four classified as having 'working-class' origins in Table 2 are in the sample because of, first, their business success and, second, their interest in activities outside their business; in Table 1 they are both classified in Group 1, and in achieving their success they have moved out of their original social class. The other two of the four are trade union organisers and appear in Group 5 of Table 1.

The educational background of members of the sample is as might be expected. Sixty per cent attended public schools and another 32 per cent went to grammar schools. Nearly one-half went up to a university, most of them to Oxford or Cambridge. About twenty or so are professionally qualified, usually in law or accountancy, often by means of articles and part-time study rather than by university attendance. One or two of the seven women substituted world travel for a university training.

The average age of the sample is fifty-six. The following table shows their age distribution.

TABLE 3   Age distribution of the sample

| Age | No. | % |
|---|---|---|
| 1. 30–9 | 6 | 8 |
| 2. 40–9 | 16 | 20 |
| 3. 50–9 | 24 | 31 |
| 4. 60–9 | 26 | 33 |
| 5. 70–9 | 5 | 6 |
| 6. 80–9 | 1 | 1 |
| 7. Total | 78 | 99[1] |

Then, as Table 4 shows, the vast majority support the Conservative Party with a greater or lesser degree of enthusiasm and involvement, to be discussed at greater length in Chapter 6 below. As one inelegantly put it, 'both parties stink', so he 'chose the lesser of two evils'. A few sought to extenuate themselves for their choice by muttering something about having a 'Liberal background', or about being 'independent', or even about voting Liberal despite their subscriptions to, and general support of, the Conservative Party and its candidates; the vote is secret, but overt support of the Conservative Party in these circles is expected and accepted.[2] It was

[1] The percentages are rounded off.

[2] Similarly small farmers in a country village may belong to the local Unionist Association but vote Labour; J. Littlejohn, *Westrigg: The Sociology of a Cheviot Parish* (Routledge & Kegan Paul, 1963) p. 107.

possible to establish the party identity of only 80 per cent of the sample. There is no reason to suppose that the party sympathies of the rest are very different, but they may be less firm in their views, and there are perhaps a few abstainers amongst them.

TABLE 4   Party allegiances

|  | No. | % |
|---|---|---|
| 1. Indicating party allegiance | 62 | 80[1] |
| 2. Conservative | 53 | 85 |
| 3. Liberal | 4 | 6 |
| 4. Labour | 5 | 8 |
| 5. Total | 62 | 99[a] |

While many have strong reservations about party politics and one of the criteria for selection of this group was their avoidance of council membership, in comparison with the general population many are very active in politics indeed – holding office in the party, canvassing, helping candidates, subscribing, mixing with the leadership and so forth.[3] The finding that some 85 per cent of a sample of people considered 'influential' in the community are committed on the side of the Conservative Party merely corroborates what is generally assumed, but it is significant none the less.[4] The predominantly class character of party politics in the municipal arena, suggested by electoral geography, is illustrated also by this finding.

[1] Percentage of sample.
[a] The percentages are rounded off.
[3] The much lower degree of political participation by most people in Bristol is suggested in R. S. Milne and H. C. Mackenzie, *Marginal Seat* (Hansard Society, 1958) pp. 14–17.
[4] A similar proportion of 'well-to-do proprietors and managers' and 'higher professionals' was found to support the Conservatives in 1951; J. Bonham, *The Middle-Class Vote* (Faber, 1954) p. 126. See also Glossop (Birch, *Small-Town Politics*, p. 106).

B

Two important aspects of the sample are, first, that on an estimate which in the absence of diligent historical research is only a crude one, 50 per cent can be classified as belonging to families established and more or less well-known in and about the city for more than one generation; second, with a few exceptions, the sample is nevertheless very homogeneous in many respects. Of the more prominent personages in the sample, a majority are linked with old Bristol families. However, much of their importance derives not merely from membership of these families as such, but also from the longstanding connection between their families and the professional, commercial or industrial firms in which they hold positions.[1] In describing members of the sample as economic and social 'notables' I have used Franco-American terminology.[2] There are one or two economic notables who are not also social notables; one or two social notables are not also economic notables. Most emphasise their economic role rather than their social prestige; or, more accurately, their economic role is essential to nearly all in maintaining their high social status.[3]

Respondents were asked to what they attributed the influence most of them realistically admitted to enjoying in the community. A great variety of replies was elicited but the next table attempts to analyse and classify most of their content. It is clear even from these highly subjective replies that many respondents themselves

[1] In an important sense, the holding of these positions is, for them, *the* social role.

[2] e.g. Daniel Halévy, *La Fin des Notables* (Grasset, Paris, 1944); Dahl, *Who Governs?*

[3] The terminological distinction between the economic, social and political roles is maintained by Bealey, *et al.*, *Constituency Politics*, p. 386. The term 'social leaders' employed by Lee (*Social Leaders*) was felt to be inappropriate here.

recognise that, though other factors are not negligible, the primary, original source of 'influence' for most is a privileged occupational start, usually with, sometimes without, an inherited privileged social position. Even much of the importance of 'contacts' and 'friends' derives from membership of leading families and firms.

TABLE 5

Factors[1] behind position of influence according to sample

|  | No. | % |
|---|---|---|
| 1. Business or professional position | 50 | 64 |
| 2. Contacts | 45 | 58 |
| 3. Friends | 26 | 33 |
| 4. Member of prominent family | 26 | 33 |
| 5. Enterprise, energy | 20 | 26 |
| 6. Philosophy of life | 16 | 21 |
| 7. Reputation, judgement, integrity | 15 | 19 |
| 8. Interest in people | 13 | 17 |
| 9. Wealth | 11 | 14 |
| 10. Upbringing, discipline, principles | 9 | 12 |
| 11. Technical or professional knowledge | 7 | 9 |

These members of established Bristol families, together with others of like status, form a tolerably recognisable and cohesive group with similar backgrounds, standards and aspirations. Studies of economic and social structure in other communities have revealed large changes in local leadership there in the past sixty years. For example, two important features have been demonstrated by studies of Cheshire by J. M. Lee, of West Country and Northern villages by W. M. Williams, of the north Midland area of Newcastle under Lyme by F. Bealey, J. Blondel and W. P. McCann, of South Wales by T. Brennan, E. W. Cooney and H. Pollins, of the Northern town of Glossop by A. H. Birch, and of

[1] Many respondents mentioned more than one factor.

the south Midland town of Banbury by Margaret Stacey.[1] First, where the landed gentry and aristocracy, with or without 'naturalised' urban wealth, were dominant they have either given up their estates altogether, departing for the metropolitan life and milder climes, or they have retreated into semi-retirement often even from local economic and social leadership – in either case surrendering local political leadership, which has quite altered there in composition and type over the past two generations. Secondly there has occurred in some of these places a reasonably clear division, owing to profound local economic changes, between the 'traditional' and the 'non-traditional' status and value systems. In Bristol, economic and social leadership has been and largely remains firmly in the hands of an urban commercial and industrial upper class of very long standing, for Bristol has been a large trading, manufacturing and urban community for many centuries. When landed magnates dominated social and political life in Cheshire in the 1880s and 1890s, typical M.P.s sitting for Bristol constituencies were local industrial magnates. They have since retired from most formal positions of political leadership even though the type at the head of the economic and social systems has remained pretty constant, the slow but continuous changes in commercial and industrial techniques and organisations being reflected in little more than constant minor modifications in the composition of the personnel;

[1] Lee, *Social Leaders*, pp. 5–7, 20, 92–102; W. M. Williams, *The Sociology of an English Village: Gosforth* (Routledge & Kegan Paul, 1956) p. 118; W. M. Williams, *A West Country Village: Ashworthy* (Routledge & Kegan Paul, 1963) pp. 197–9; Bealey *et al.*, *Constituency Politics*, pp. 25–8, 66, 107; Brennan, *et al.*, *Social Change in South-West Wales*, pp. 28, 108–10, 187; Birch, *Small-Town Politics*, pp. 23–31, 120, 130, 186; Stacey, *Tradition and Change*, pp. 15, 36, 52.

thence the common values and high degree of unity of 'old' and 'new' elements in the sample, since the 'native' status and value systems in Bristol are less 'traditional' and more absorptive and adaptable than those in, say, Banbury.[1] Their position is often defined by social status, but also by role; and their influence flows not merely from ascriptive rights, but also from socially esteemed achievement. The ancient alliance between land-based gentry and the urban commercial and professional upper classes often continues to be symbolised in the large ex-urban residencies, not too far removed, in the social connections and in the weakness for country pursuits of many of the wealthy city people; but it is the urban, moderately innovating contribution which has long been the dominant, not the subordinate, element.

They live in a few well-defined areas inside and outside the city; it is not true, as one claimed, that 'all the top people live outside the city', but during the past hundred years there has been an important exodus into the neighbouring countryside mainly of north Somerset. Just over half the sample, including many but by no means all the top businessmen, live outside Bristol. However, at least three-quarters even of these live within about eight miles or less of the city centre, and most of the rest live little further away and nearly all, as we shall see, continue to identify closely with the city. Many enjoy close mutual social relationships, as personal friends, as club acquaintances, as members of boards of directors, or on the magistrates' bench; they are associated together in people's minds – they are invited to run the Cathedral Appeal Fund and so forth. Of the thirty-one non-council patrons or committee members of the Appeal Fund, twelve are included in the

[1] Stacey, *Tradition and Change*, pp. 15, 36, 52.

sample. Some of the families have considerable rami-
fications and interconnect through marriage, within and
without the sample, and a wedding at this level is hailed
by the local Press as the 'City's wedding of the year'.
Two or three people likened Bristol to a 'village'. Clearly
a city of 430,000 is not a village, but if one's main
relationships are primarily with a few high-status
people, then one may feel one is living in a 'village'.
And, as in a village, the various families are so well
known to each other that backbiting sometimes occurs
between them; Bristol was said to be 'a gossipy parochial
village, where there are inborn jealousies between
families'.[1] One man quoted with approval the dictum,
he said, of a civil servant, who described Bristol as being
run by a 'democratic oligarchy' – the phrase is im-
precise, but the implications are fairly clear. A great
deal of the social and economic leadership[2] is in the
hands of members of well-established families, prominent in one way or another in the life of the community
for two or more generations, together with others of
similar background and origins. This is consistent with
the fact that amongst the latter are one or two of the
most prominent people in the sample, who are to some
extent 'outsiders' in the social-status sense, and are
either longstanding immigrants or have made their own
way from more humble beginnings.

Many members of that half of the group which does

[1] Interesting comparisons might be made with some aspects of
village life; for example, the acceptance amongst members of the
group of group-judgements upon various of its members repeated
to the interviewer. Cf. Williams, *A West Country Village*, p. 184.
For the exclusive intimacy between members of upper-class
families in another village, see Williams, *Sociology of an English
Village*, p. 100.
[2] But what exactly this implies in concrete consequences to
others has not been satisfactorily determined.

not derive from established, well-known Bristol families, though often lacking the more intimate interconnections (and a few hardly connect at all), in a variety of ways do interact with, and share, the outlooks of the more patrician element. This judgement is supported by a more rigorous analysis of 'sub-groups' – professional people, members of established Bristol families, those designated as originating in the 'upper' social classes – with regard to attitudes specifically towards the Council and participation on the Council. Such analysis shows a very close correspondence of views between the sub-groups and the sample as a whole (see Chapter 6, below). Moreover, this is not a one-way process; the 'patricians' themselves come more than half-way to meet the executive/professional/immigrant type in mastering skills, and in the day-to-day management of business or professional affairs. The patrician half of the sample are part, not of an aloof aristocracy, but of a deeply involved group of modern notables, with a high regard for business values and businessmen.[1] It is important to notice here that nearly all those consulted about the composition of the sample are themselves relatively recent 'immigrants' to Bristol and therefore not so liable as natives may be to mistake an aura of mere tradition for real standing.

A few of the respondents are retired or semi-retired, but even these tend to keep a foothold, a directorship or two, in the business world. A few are women who hold no paid job. But in general most of the sample have high places in professional occupations or in business

---

[1] Anthony Sampson has noticed that the English aristocracy has not merely continued to give its historical welcome to new commercial and industrial wealth but takes a pride in its involvement in the money-making processes (*Anatomy of Britain Today* (Hodder & Stoughton, 1965) p. 562).

firms. There is a good deal of overlapping. Several of the professional men have directorships in business firms; several of the businessmen have professional qualifications and experience. The line between business and professional ideologies and interests seems very blurred. Many are mainly preoccupied with a particular chairmanship or managing directorship, giving subsidiary attention to a cluster of directorships and interests in other firms, sometimes similar, sometimes quite different.

Though very frequently the business or professional interests of these people are chiefly local, they are often also at least partly regional, or metropolitan, or national, or even international in nature.[1] A number of medium and small businesses in the city have been taken over in recent years and, though much of the local character, personnel and organisation may be retained, their ultimate headquarters are now in London. A chartered accountant said, 'Client after client is now controlled from London.'[2] Or a man may have directorships in firms of world renown outside his own original business and with headquarters in London; or again, some of these companies, founded and still based in Bristol, have become regionally, nationally and sometimes internationally known, with corresponding wide-flung interests and organisation; whilst, for some of the older men and women, public or voluntary service on

[1] These developments are not peculiar to Bristol, of course. For example, see Sampson, *Anatomy*, p. 554.

[2] Presumably, depending on the circumstances, with the (delayed) effect of changing the status of (some) former proprietors to that of managers. The process has not gone so far as to be an adequate explanation for the withdrawal of economic notables from political leadership in Bristol, whatever its adequacy in Newcastle under Lyme; Bealey, *et al.*, *Constituency Politics*, p. 390.

the national stage looms even larger than business. In all these instances there is constant intercourse with the metropolis, a two-hour Pullman-ride away, upon which acquaintanceships within the group are made or maintained; sometimes there is traffic with other regional centres, and even abroad. Plane travel, public or private, is commonplace, and two or three find a permanent *pied-à-terre* in London convenient. The following tables illustrate something of this mobility and wide-flung interest. It will be seen that many are more accustomed to travel to and from London than within and about Bristol, whilst journeys around the region and in the provinces are quite common.

TABLE 6   Type of travel entailed by job and other interests

|  | No. | %[1] |
|---|---|---|
| 1. Extensive travel in Bristol | 33 | 42 |
| 2. Little travel in Bristol | 45 | 58 |
| 3. Visit provincial centres | 10 | 13 |
| 4. Regional travel usual | 17 | 22 |
| 5. International trips very common | 7 | 9 |

TABLE 7   Visits to London almost entirely on public, business and professional matters

|  | No. | % |
|---|---|---|
| 1. Up to 4 per year | 8 | 10 |
| 2. 4–12 per year | 15 | 19 |
| 3. 13–50 per year | 34 | 44 |
| 4. 2–3 days a week or fortnight | 20 | 26 |
| 5. Long stay at a time | 1 | 1 |
| 6. Total | 78 | 100 |

Is it then quite unrealistic to discuss service on a local Council with such a group? Not at all. It is true that one or two – younger, more recent immigrants – denied any

[1] More than one answer was given sometimes.

B 2

feeling of identification with the city, but most gloried in their close association with, and their 'roots' in, the local society and its history. That long-established roots in the city are instrumental in gaining entry to the group of accepted 'influentials' has already been illustrated by the fact that half belong to well-known city-families. But 'roots', or long associations with the community, also imply long residence in or near the city. Fifty-six per cent have lived here all their lives, another 22 per cent over twenty years, and only 8 people, or 10 per cent of the sample, less than ten years.[1] Seventy-one, or 91 per cent of the sample, agree that Bristol has provided the focus for their lives and careers, many most emphatically. A few stipulated that they identified also with the surrounding region. Two highly placed men who for many years at one stage in their careers had been in charge of north-country branches for their firms nevertheless maintained their homes here. The chairman of one of the largest and most dominant companies in the city, admitting that 'the focus of my company job is really in London', nevertheless says, 'I should be sorry if I had to go'; so he spends more than half his time in London but lives in Bristol. Another, not the least urbane, wealthy, highly educated and travelled member of the sample, contrasts the ethics of Bristol businessmen with those of London – the latter is 'a haven of shysters'. An accountant complains that London businessmen 'think only of profit and loss, not

[1] The figures are not strictly comparable, as half the sample live outside the city limits, but the sample of electors in Bristol North-East used by Milne and Mackenzie in 1951 looks more mobile residentially. R. S. Milne and M. C. Mackenzie, *Straight Fight* (Hansard Society, 1954) p. 161. A random sample of people in top jobs in the city would undoubtedly produce a higher proportion of 'immigrants' – and of less socially active people. Cf. Birch, *Small-Town Politics*, p. 116.

human values'. Even the most 'metropolitan' or 'national' still find room amongst their extensive pre-occupations for a close concern with the fortunes of the community with which in a real sense they continue to identify.[1] This loyalty is perhaps not so narrowly intense as amongst some of the more circumscribed, within and without the sample, but it often gains a new pungency and point from the width of experience of affairs elsewhere.

It is worth pursuing the problem of identification with the local community a little further. Over half (53 per cent) state emphatically that they have never thought of going to live elsewhere. 'My whole life is tied up with Bristol,' says one. 'I'm a Bristolian by nature,' says a second. 'I've been round the world and there is no place I prefer,' says another. 'Being in Bristol is like being on holiday,' smiles yet another. According to an immigrant, 'I'm happier here than I've ever been elsewhere – it provides a full and satisfying life.' A self-made man says contentedly, 'I've done very well here and made a lot of money – I've no incentive to go.' Another 18 per cent says they have 'not really' thought of going, which usually indicates a temporary unsettled frame of mind at the end of the war. Two men – in the church – regard themselves as wholly at the disposal of higher authority. While a handful have in the past considered tempting offers of opportunities elsewhere, only four people, or 5 per cent of the sample, are at present actively considering departing, or would welcome the chance to go if it came up. In accounting for this immobility, 55 per

[1] Unlike the modern industrialist 'Lord A' living outside Banbury but with no roots in the locality; Stacey, *Tradition and Change*, pp. 17, 36. It is certainly not true of the Bristol sample that the west end of London is its 'town centre'; Stacey, *Tradition and Change*, p. 154. Cf. Lee, *Social Leaders*, pp. 42, 86, 93; Birch, *Small-Town Politics*, pp. 34–8, 116; and Bealey, *et al.*, *Constituency Politics*, pp. 53–4.

cent laid particular stress on their job, 22 per cent mentioned their 'roots', a third referred to the binding character of their social relationships or friendships, and a third also dwelt upon the holding power of Bristol's pleasant physical environment. The total picture is one of great immobility and of attachment to the area.

Additional measures of local interest are the extent to which people read the local Press and their motives for doing so. There are two locally published papers, owned by the same company. The evening paper, the more local of the two, is an established success with a large circulation within and beyond the city. It regards itself as 'independent with a slight Tory bias'. The latter shows in its Rhodesian line, but it has 'progressive' views on numerous non-party matters – the morality of circuses, capital punishment, fornication and so forth, and in the past has been sympathetic to C.N.D. The morning paper is more regional and conservative in character, and has recently extended its readership by adopting a more aggressive and less inhibited tone than formerly. Of the sample, only 6 per cent read neither paper, while 38 per cent read both; a third read the evening paper only, a fifth read the morning paper only.[1] 'Read' is a very flexible term. No direct observation of newspaper-reading habits could be made, but the answers to my questions made clear that 'reading' varies from a cursory glance, maybe only at the copy provided at work, to a rather close daily scrutiny of a

[1] Compare readership of the local Press amongst a sample of the general population. Maud Report, III, *The Local Government Elector*, p. 31, table 42. More of the sample of notables were found to read the local Press than were found to do so amongst the electorate in Bristol North-East in 1955. Then only 40 per cent of the Conservatives in the constituency read the *Evening Post* regularly. (The subsequent death of the *Evening World* hardly affects the comparison.) Milne and Mackenzie, *Marginal Seat*, p. 101.

variety of items. At a rough estimate, perhaps as many as a half come into the latter category, not much more than a tenth in the former, and the rest fall between these positions.

The major reasons given for following the local Press appear in the next table. Despite the acerbity of some of the comments about these papers – 'ghastly', 'sensationalise the news' – the great majority find something of interest in their contents, and many actively approve of one or both of them. Although one man does say he looks for the latest national news in their pages, and some of the business news if of a 'national' character, it should be observed that the group's very general and close interest in the local Press is overwhelmingly a *local* one. A typical comment is, 'I read the *Post* to find out what's going on – because I'm *involved* in what's going on.' This evidence illustrates graphically the point that however national, metropolitan or regional are many of the concerns of these people, the vast majority also feel closely identified with local events. They are by no means aloof, nor without the time to take a keen interest in local affairs. Had this finding been different, it would, of course, have been difficult to sustain the view that these people are in a real sense people of influence in an identifiable 'community' called Bristol.[1]

It did not appear during the interviews that residence beyond the city limits made any significant difference to

[1] Though many of the same trends towards the functionalisation and delocalisation of life described by Rose (*Politics i n England*, pp. 178–81) and noted in Glossop by Birch (*Smal.-Town Politics*, pp. 184–91) and in South Wales by Brennan, *et al* (*Social Change in South West Wales*, p. 190) are also evident in Bristol, their impact upon the quality of local life here has so far been less abrupt or less apparent; perhaps people of the type represented by the sample play some small part in bridging the communications gap.

TABLE 8    Reasons for attention to the local press

|  | No. | %[1] |
|---|---|---|
| 1. General local interest – 'What's going on' | 35 | 45 |
| 2. Business reasons | 32 | 41 |
| 3. Close relevance to own activities other than business | 10 | 13 |
| 4. Social – deaths, friends' activities | 30 | 38 |
| 5. Idle entertainment, spectator interest | 10 | 13 |
| 6. Church news | 3 | 4 |
| 7. Sport | 3 | 4 |

the sentiments commonly held by the sample about Bristol or about service on the local Council, or to their identification with the city community. While it was amongst the group of non-residents that the one or two were to be found who protested their lack of interest in, or identification with, Bristol and therefore their indifference to service on Bristol's Council, this was still very rare, and analysis of replies by the country-dwellers to questions on reasons for avoiding Council service shows that the pattern of responses was very similar to that of the replies from the sample as a whole. They identify with a community the great core of which is the city because many actually lived within it when younger and live very close now, their business and social interests still largely focus there, and there are sufficient of their own kind resident within the city to preserve them from feelings of alienation.

One of the criteria of selection of the sample was considerable activity in voluntary work, and the sample appears to measure up to this requirement. The list of organisations in which they are or have very recently

[1] More than one reason was sometimes given and therefore total percentages add up to more than 100. This is true of subsequent tables also.

been active is formidable, and Table 9 gives merely a selection of those most frequently mentioned and of most apparent interest. So far as it has been possible to check, the information given appears to be substantially correct, but more especially where important positions are involved; thus, all who are J.P.s said so; all who are members of the university council said so; but only a few of those who are members of the university court (which has no power, is large and meets rarely) mentioned it. A very common kind of activity is in connection with business or professional organisations – the Chamber of Commerce, trade associations, the Confederation of British Industries, the Institute of Directors, the professional institutes and so forth. This activity can be local or national in character. Then there are public positions, like membership of advisory committees, of the Commonwealth Development Corporation, of hospital boards, employment committees, industrial training-boards, the magistrates' bench, as well as appointments as county deputy lieutenants, sheriffs, commissioners of income tax and the like. A third important category comprises welfare and social work – school and college governorships, the university court and council, charitable institutions (in which Bristol is very rich), church organisations, social service bodies, boys' clubs, the Scouts, the Y.W.C.A., organisations to help the elderly, the incapacitated and the ill. Some of these may involve national committee work. Then there are social organisations such as the Masons, the Savages, the Territorials, the British Legion, political and other clubs; and, fifthly, *ad hoc* activities like membership of a Royal Commission or service on the local Cathedral Fund appeal.[1]

[1] For fairly typical collections of memberships and offices, see the postscript to Chapter 1 above.

TABLE 9   Membership of selected organisations or offices

|  | No. | %[1] |
|---|---|---|
| 1. Magistrate | 31 | 40 |
| 2. Chamber of Commerce | 27 | 35 |
| 3. Merchant Venturers Society | 20 | 26 |
| 4. Hospital boards, committees | 18 | 23 |
| 5. British Legion | 16 | 21 |
| 6. Rotary | 14 | 18 |
| 7. Parochial church council | 13 | 17 |
| 8. Cathedral appeal | 12 | 15 |
| 9. University council | 11 | 14 |
| 10. Masons | 7 | 9 |
| 11. Institute of Directors | 7 | 9 |
| 12. Commissioners of Income Tax | 7 | 9 |
| 13. Confederation of British Industries | 7 | 9 |
| 14. Law Society | 4 | 5 |

Members of the sample are, typically, active if they belong to some such body or fill some such post. 'If I can't be active, I don't join', or 'One shouldn't be a passenger – I don't like wasting time', they say. At some stage they hold office, as chairman, president or secretary, in organisations or branches to which they belong. Some of these positions are much more demanding than others; the presidency of the village British Legion branch is often little more than honorific, but the chairmanship of the magistrates' bench is very different in its demands, and in many cases the hours consumed by these activities are very full ones. It was difficult for many of my respondents to make an accurate assessment of the time they put into such work. It is not altogether easy for, say, a parson to divide his pastoral duties from other interests, or for a businessman clearly to distinguish between his work as chairman of the company and service as a member of a committee of the

[1] Some belong to more than one.

Confederation of British Industries. Service on the Bristol bench of magistrates comes in lumps of a week per quarter, whilst the presidency of the Chamber of Commerce entails exceptionally heavy inroads on time and energy for a year or so.

Sixty-seven members of the sample gave information which could be translated into terms of hours per week. On the average, they spent something like eleven hours a week in voluntary service different from, and in addition to, the direct demands made upon them by their jobs. The Government Social Survey found that councillors on all types of councils spend an average of fifty-two hours per month on council, committee or party meetings and other preparations for council and committee meetings, and on electors' problems and on associated organisations, which is closely comparable to the eleven hours per week given by my sample to their non-council voluntary activities. Moreover, the government survey shows that while county borough councillors spend more time than the average on council work, councillors of the social class from which my sample is mainly drawn – big employers, managers, professional people, the well educated and highly paid – tend to spend rather less time than the average on their council work than councillors of other social background, and quite a lot of councillors spend a good deal less time than the average on council duties.[1] The numbers of organisations joined by councillors and by members of the sample are very comparable, and far exceed the average proclivity for joining bodies amongst the general public. The propensity to join is more developed in the higher socio-economic groups.[2]

The average amount of time spent on voluntary

[1] Maud Report, II 93, table 3.1; p. 102, table 3.11.
[2] Ibid. II 185–6.

activities conceals wide variations, as the next table shows. Despite the variations, the main point seems to be established – that the voluntary burden, in terms of time, accepted by the sample, is quite comparable to the average sacrifice of time entailed for members of socio-economic group one by membership even of a county borough council. For men in some offices – President of the Chamber of Commerce, Master of a Society and so forth – the burden is greater, and these and some others give up time and attention equivalent to the sacrifices of party leaders and chairmen of important council committees.

TABLE 10

Time spent on voluntary activities – hours per week

|  | *No.* | % |
|---|---|---|
| 1. 5 or less | 15 | 22 |
| 2. 6–10 | 26 | 39 |
| 3. 11–15 | 10 | 15 |
| 4. 16–20 | 11 | 16 |
| 5. over 20 | 5 | 7 |
| 6. Total | 67 | 99 |

# CHAPTER 3

# *Reasons Given for not Standing for the Council*

How, then, do these people explain why they do not serve on the local authority of the city in which they work and with which they so largely identify and in whose affairs they take so deep and active an interest? Over two-thirds (73 per cent) have never given the possibility of their joining the Council any thought – compared with 94 per cent of a sample of the general population.[1] Only 9 people, or 11 per cent of the sample, have ever been councillors in any local authority.[2] This latter figure represents a much larger proportion than one would find among a random sample of the population, which might seem odd since a major criterion of selection of the sample was their avoidance of council service, but when it is recalled that these people are energetic, well regarded, of high economic and social status, and that most play some part in politics, it is less surprising that a few should at some time have joined a council. Rather it highlights the problem why such people do not more habitually participate more intensively in local government.

[1] Maud Report, III 138, table 184.
[2] Two are ex-parish councillors; one has sat on a rural district council; one has been on both a rural district council and a county council; five are Bristol ex-councillors of various vintages.

Respondents first gave their own reasons for not becoming local councillors, or for ceasing to be so. They were then asked to pick, out of a list of twenty-three potential grounds for non-participation, any that they felt had been of importance to themselves. The next table shows the reasons most commonly mentioned and Table 12 amalgamates certain categories and eliminates overlapping.

TABLE 11

Reasons given for not seeking to join the local Council

|  | *No.* | % |
|---|---|---|
| 1. Excessive calls on time | 55 | 71 |
| 2. Other activities preferred | 33 | 42 |
| 3. Dislike close party attachment and discipline | 30 | 38 |
| 4. Dislike party politics in local government | 23 | 29 |
| 5. Business comes first | 20 | 26 |
| 6. Dislike elections | 20 | 26 |
| 7. Work or position requires non-partisan appearance | 19 | 24 |
| 8. Awkward times of meetings | 19 | 24 |
| 9. Poor quality of councillors | 18 | 23 |
| 10. Doubts on personal suitability | 16 | 21 |
| 11. Cumbrous machine | 11 | 14 |
| 12. Job needs not predictable | 10 | 13 |
| 13. Frustration by inefficiency | 9 | 12 |
| 14. Different pattern of activity developed | 8 | 10 |
| 15. Not sufficiently individual | 8 | 10 |
| 16. Dislike of publicity | 8 | 10 |
| 17. Was not invited | 7 | 9 |
| 18. Council lacks power | 7 | 9 |

A comparison between the unprompted and the prompted answers indicates that no important bias was introduced by the prompting, which served mainly to extract fuller replies. Occasionally it suggested something new, unmentioned without prompting; for example, the notion that respondents might dislike 'wielding power over others'. Nobody said so without prompting. When prompted, most passed it over in silence, presumably either because it did not apply to them, or because they missed its implications. A few paused to express surprise at so novel an idea, or to say that on the contrary they enjoy exercising power over others, pointing out that they have done so, long and

TABLE 12   Major reasons given for not seeking
to join the local Council

|  | No. | % |
|---|---|---|
| 1. Excessive time required | 60 | 77 |
| 2. Dislike party politics in local government | 58 | 68 |
| 3. Other activities preferred | 33 | 42 |
| 4. Low efficiency in local government | 27 | 35 |

continuously. The notion caused discomfort to some; one argued that somebody has to wield power and that he not only uses it with a sense of humility, but also does more good with it than others. Another said it is not power he is wielding when he takes decisions he knows to be right. One refused to be a J.P. because of the power implications of the office – 'I've spent thirty years of my life judging people in business, and didn't want to do more of that.' A clergyman wished he could say he does not enjoy exercising power but confessed that he does. Two or three (4 per cent) did, when prompted, include a revulsion from the exercise of power among their reasons for not becoming councillors – in the words of one, 'I prefer to live and let live' – but none could with logic do so and retain his other posts. In sum, therefore, prompting had only this kind of marginal effect and imparted no great bias to the main results of the inquiry.

Tables 11 and 12 show that the reason most frequently given by the sample for not becoming local councillors is that council membership levies too heavy a toll upon time, which respondents cannot afford to give. Many emphasise the primacy of their duties to their job, their firm, their career or their profession. One man described his profession, in a Calvinistic phrase, as his 'calling'. Another says 'one is dedicated' to one's job, and a third, 'the business is always in one's mind, seven days a week'. And so, the argument runs, if they put their occupation first, as they should, they cannot also be adequate councillors. Several referred to specific examples of men whose membership of the Council led, according to the group folk-lore, to the dire neglect of their businesses. Most of these cases occurred in the distant past, and evidently influenced respondents as they established their life-patterns at the outset of their careers. One or two more recent examples have served only to confirm the wisdom of their earlier decision. Many men in the sample look upon the meticulous pursuit of their occupation, no matter what, almost as a trust, an obligation to the firm, to the industry or profession, and even to the community. According to one prominent businessman, in doing so he is 'doing as much for the community as anybody'. This feeling is equally as strong amongst the 'immigrants' as amongst those with old Bristol connections. Deep concern and interest in one's career may make it a formidable competitor to council service. In contrast, many working-class councillors get little satisfaction from their occupations.[1]

It is important to notice, also, that the seven people who have served on a rural district council or on Bristol Council itself all emphasised excessive claims on their

[1] Maud Report, II 150, table 4.13.

time as a dominant reason for giving up their representative status. Primarily it was with the demands of business that the competition was felt, but, also, in three instances, with other kinds of voluntary work. The claims of their local authority were growing or threatening to do so, or its demands had already made unforeseen inroads upon the attention which they and their business colleagues felt should be paid to their jobs. They made other points, too, but the time factor was most generally mentioned by this group, as by the rest of the sample.

Later, respondents were asked if they thought that people like them[1] were more or less active in local government fifty years ago and, if there have been any changes, why? Table 13 shows their replies. The emphasis on the 'time' factor is repeated; it is generally felt that the growth in size of firms, the rise of the competitive managerial class at the expense of the leisured proprietor, forcing the latter to adopt a similar way of life, and the general demands of modern society have reduced the reserves of time and energy that this class could formerly consume in the service of local government, which itself has become more demanding. Thus the head of one world-renowned firm said, 'My father [his predecessor] was a councillor – but he was at business only between 11.30 and 4.30.' One man referred to the shortage of domestic servants; others mentioned the interval required for them to 'unwind' when on holiday; another commented on today's 'ghastly pressure to make a living'; and a woman noted how young men at the bar or in commerce now 'work at top speed'.

There are, besides, the complaints made about the awkward times of meetings, but these are made only by a minority and are frequently another way of

[1] If applicable, their forebears.

complaining about the total consumption of time;[1] even when prompted, some three-quarters of the sample refused to shelter behind the rather obvious alibi that times of council and committee meetings are too

TABLE 13   Predecessors of fifty years ago
and their participation in local government

|  | No. | % |
|---|---|---|
| 1. More active fifty years ago | 49 | 63 |
| 2. More active now | 1 | 1 |
| 3. No change | 16 | 21 |
| 4. Increased burden of business | 32 | 41 |
| 5. Less leisure | 10 | 12 |
| 6. More working-class competition | 12 | 15 |
| 7. Growth in local party politics | 12 | 15 |
| 8. Increased burden of council work | 4 | 5 |
| 9. Decline in local authority power | 3 | 4 |
| 10. More authority in business | 2 | 3 |

difficult for them. It is probably true that evening meetings would inconvenience more in this sample than would be helped. Professional people who need to be on call at least in normal working-hours are no doubt most disadvantaged at present. Businessmen who cited the unpredictability of demands on their time by their jobs probably would not be much helped by shifting council meetings to the evenings. It is possible that holding them in the very late afternoon would suit rather more people than present arrangements do. But any changes of this sort would be of very marginal effect. The reality of the complaints about consumption of time as such is illustrated by the unanimity of the ex-councillors on this point, by the circumstantial elaboration of the needs of professions and businesses in regard to their total time-

[1] This is not to deny the point in the Maud Report, II 105, that times of meetings may well affect the kind of councillor recruited.

needs and by references to the value of the greater predictability and convenience of alternative uses of their time. Family life and much voluntary activity can be made to adapt to business demands, but council work rarely can. The investigations of the Social Survey on behalf of the Maud Committee also found that the various groups – councillors, ex-councillors, electors – make considerable play of the voracious consumption of time by council work as a main disincentive to participation. Thus 23 per cent of the Social Survey sample of electors gave lack of time as their main reason for not wishing to be a councillor.[1] And it is of particular interest to us that it was found that 39 per cent of socio-economic group one – large employers, managers and professionals – put this factor first.[2] As the Report suggests, lack of time 'may be a real and important deterrent to participation in voluntary council work'.[3] The evidence therefore suggests that recommendations such as those made by the Maud Committee which would cut the amount of time that councillors must spend in Council, on committees and in preparation for meetings, would contribute to encouraging people represented by this sample to join in local government.

And yet for a great part of the sample the plea of pressure of time cannot be accepted as a sufficient and conclusive reason why they do not take part in local government, and indeed very few leave the argument at that. We have seen above how big a commitment, an average of eleven hours a week, they do accept in voluntary affairs outside their work. This is far more than most people devote to such activity – only 9 per cent of the Maud sample claimed to spend more than twenty hours a month on 'organisations', which were

[1] Maud Report, III 122, table 169; also I 141, 144.
[2] Ibid. III 124, table 171.          [3] Ibid. III 159.

very widely defined, and only 56 per cent of the 'joiners' had attended meetings of their organisations in the previous month.[1] In other words, the sample of 'notables' has 'spare' time, but they choose to spend it in ways other than in service on the local council.[2] Again the Social Survey follows a similar line of reasoning, based on rather different evidence. It points out that there are large variations in the time spent on council work by high-status councillors, indicating that some have adapted the situation to their needs, whilst the abandonment of council work by ex-councillors seems to be only negatively related, if at all, to the time spent on council duties.[3] These active notables don't spend their 'spare' time asleep, or in the garden, or in front of the television set, but as members, chairmen or presidents of a variety of bodies, engaged in voluntary work of some sort. They make, in most cases, a quite deliberate choice between competing alternatives. Tables 11 and 12 show that over 40 per cent explicitly state that they find such work preferable to council service. How then do they explain this behaviour?

In Tables 11 and 12 an unfavourable attitude to party politics in local government is evident, and indeed it ran through many interviews as a sort of refrain, much more so than complaints about demands on time. Indeed, only 14 (19 per cent) did not at some stage in the interview make some derogatory remark about politics in local government, ranging from passing mild regret to bitter condemnation. In one way or another over two-thirds of the sample mentioned party politics

[1] Maud Report, III 116–17. Those who claim to spend time on their organisations on average spend only 13½ hours a month upon them; table 116. And the more highly educated groups are the greatest joiners (p. 115).

[2] Cf. comment in Maud Report, I 144, para. 156.

[3] Maud Report, II 104, 248.

as at least one reason why they refuse to participate and for many it is the major one, or the first to be mentioned.

The findings of the Social Survey on behalf of the Maud Committee appear somewhat ambiguous on this point. Of the sample of electors only 3 per cent say they dislike the party system in local government, only 1 per cent give it as a reason for not going on the Council, and only 3 per cent say that making local government non-political is the one thing that would make local government attractive.[1] Moreover, only 8 per cent of the sample of councillors find politics on the Council frustrating, and a mere 4 per cent of councillors know of people kept off the Council by dislike of party politics;[2] and ex-councillors blame time factors more than politics both for their own decision to give up and for preventing others joining the Council.[3] It is this kind of evidence which influences the report of the Committee, when discussing the effects of politics on the quality of local government and local councillors, to remain satisfied with the truth that no administrative decree is likely to reduce the incidence of politics at the local level, whilst regretting the deterrent effect of party politics upon 'independent-minded people'.[4] It is not clear who these latter are. However, the Social Survey yields evidence that to some social groups politics in local government is more distasteful than to others. While only 3 per cent of electors believe that making local government 'non-political' is the most important change to attract people into it, 10 per cent of socio-economic group 1 do so.[5] Besides, 28 per cent of those

[1] Maud Report, III 69, table 98; p. 122, table 169; p. 129, table 177.          [2] Ibid. II 141, 203.

[3] Ibid. II 258, 280–1. They are less happy about politics than councillors though.          [4] Ibid. I 145.

[5] Ibid. III 129, table 177; p. 131, table 179; p. 158.

members of this socio-economic group who are ex-councillors blame frustration by the party system or other aspects of local government for their abandonment of council membership, as against 21 per cent of all ex-councillors.[1] Amongst councillors, too, employers, managers and professional men are more hostile to organised political parties on Councils than are councillors of other social backgrounds.[2] These findings suggest a relationship between high socio-economic status and repugnance for local party politics, and this is in line with the evidence that an even larger proportion of my own more narrowly selected group of active high-status people share this repugnance.

'Politics' covers a variety of sins. Mostly it refers to the carrying of national party loyalties and ideologies – irrelevantly, they believe – into local government matters through the organisation of local politics, on and off the Council, by branches of the national parties; it is said that councillors 'use local politics for national ends and for the furtherance of their political aims'. Many believe that party conflict entails inefficiency, time-wasting, wrong decisions and dishonesty. One denounced political ambition and 'political intrigue', whilst another commented that councillors 'score off each other to establish the party image, so that the needs of the community take second place to political party needs'. Yet another distasteful aspect is the discussion in committee and Council, referred to as 'wrangling'; some are quite offended by 'rude and malevolent abuse' exchanged between politicians, who, it seems, delight in 'scratching other people's eyes out'. A number find repugnant the prospect of enduring elections and public argument. Many dislike the implications of party discipline; for

[1] Maud Report, II 261, table 9.25.
[2] Ibid. II 209, table 7.16; p. 211, table 7.20.

example, the intellectual dishonesty entailed by strict adherence to a party line. Some quoted examples of councillors confessing in private to opinions not reflected in their public speeches and votes. One man observed, out of close personal knowledge, 'M.P.s become corrupted – they become not very nice people.' In any case, party discipline would excessively confine individual initiative by the collective or leadership's will. Thus several claimed they lacked the necessary qualities to be a councillor, since they could not pledge themselves to see eye to eye and to vote with the party they chose, which made them 'bad politicians'. Such an attitude is common even amongst those having quite a close attachment to, and even office in, the Conservative Party organisation in or outside the city. Many expressed impatience with a situation where the parties alternate in power and with their competing group-doctrines and changes of committee chairmen bring instability and inefficiency to city policy. Respondents, above all, feel that reasonable men faced with a problem can analyse it into its component parts and, with the goal of community welfare as a sure guide, can all agree on the best solution, and that party dogma, intellectual dishonesty and ambition are primarily to blame for division and confusion.

Yet another 'political' obstacle to joining the Council is the feeling by about a quarter that their professional or business or public position would be compromised by open association with a partisan body. A number of J.P.s in the sample lament the alleged introduction of party allegiances into relationships on the Bench by councillor J.P.s. Clergymen emphasise their need to preserve a reputation for non-partisanship, while a large retail-store manager believes his business success depends in large measure on avoiding public avowals on both religion and politics. It is, however, mainly professional men who think that their business or social relationships might be impaired by open party-identification. That relatively few of the total sample entertain this view – and it was on the prompt list – emphasises the common recognition and understanding of the main outlines of the social structure in Bristol. As more than one respondent pointed out, actual participation in a party-dominated Council would make little difference because everybody knows that the employing class are Conservative anyway.[1] One businessman and Conservative office-holder described council politics in stark ideological and class terms: 'Citizen councillors are prompted by capitalistic motives – to stop the Labour crusade for Socialism.' In the light of the general importance of party as an objection to council service, the common failure to look on public party-identification as a problem is rather striking.

Nor did anybody suggest that he was influenced by the Citizens' position as the 'normal' minority party in post-war Bristol, leaving the Labour Party in control of the Council for thirteen of the twenty years from 1945 to 1964. Indeed, the commonly held view in the city, despite this situation, that the locus of political power does alternate is supported by the fact that the Citizens were in control between 1959 and 1962, and by 1964–5 were clearly on their way back to the power they regained in 1967. There is no evidence that, had all else remained the same, attitudes to council participation would have been radically different if the Citizens had more frequently been in control. Mere party attitudes

[1] It has been suggested that in Newcastle under Lyme large employers are inhibited from standing because as Conservatives they would be embarrassed in a Labour constituency. Bealey, *et al.*, *Constituency Politics*, p. 399.

as such to Labour's superiority appear to have little influence. Labour's qualified electoral predominance is of significance in interpreting the attitudes of the notables to participation only within the total local political and social context, and only for its contribution to the conditions of equality and competition within the political system; in a sense, of course, the rise of the Labour Party and the conditions surrounding it permeate the whole interpretation appearing in Chapter 9.

Criticism of the efficiency of the local Council, quite apart from the alleged degrading effects of party, are made, according to Table 12, by over a third of the sample, in explaining why they refuse to become councillors. The machine is said to be cumbrous, restrictive of the individual, time-wasting, boring, frustrating and, in the event, of little effect despite much effort. Criticism is directed at red tape, the bureaucratic framework and the poor relations a few feel to subsist between officials and councillors; but the chief target is the over-all set-up, designed supposedly to meet the needs of representative local government – the committees, the discussion, the subordination of the expert, and the consequent expenditure of time, the compromises and the mistakes. As several put it, the Council is avoided because it is run insufficiently like a business. Possible improvements could not be thoroughly explored in the interview, but those which might lead especially to smaller committees, meeting less frequently, or to greater independence for the officials, or even the appointment of a town manager, were desired by the few who expatiated on the problem. One even looked back to co-opting 'top people' (without party ties) as aldermen. The implications of these answers, like others mentioned in this chapter, will be explored in Chapter 9 below.

Table 11 suggests that many of the sample have less confidence in councillors' abilities than they have in their own. Amongst the fifth who say that they themselves lacked some quality necessary in a councillor are included people who are really criticising councillors rather than themselves, when, for example, they confess to not having the 'gift of the gab', and it includes other men who have long left their feelings of inadequacy behind with their youth. Consequently these findings roughly accord with the Social Survey results, which show 32 per cent of the general public, but only 11 per cent of the employer and professional classes, admitting now to some feelings of incompetence.[1]

It will be noticed that seven gave as a reason for not becoming a councillor that they had never been asked to do so. Asked directly whether they had ever been invited to stand, 56 per cent said 'No'. The rest had been approached with varying degrees of insistence; of these over three-quarters had responded incisively in the negative leaving only 9 per cent who had both been approached and had stood for local election. Considering that these people are well-known, experienced men of affairs, closely interested in the community, often politically active, it might at first seem odd that over half are not approached at all to become local candidates. But it is also clear that overtures are made to people of this sort much more frequently than amongst the general population of whom only 3 per cent report such approaches.[2] Moreover, several classed as not being invited to join a council have been asked to stand as parliamentary candidates. This high rate of approach is indicative of others' assessment of the people in the sample, and of their role in the social and the political

[1] Maud Report, III 122, table 169; p. 124, table 171.
[2] Maud Report, III p. 138, table 183.

systems. The rate of refusals to such soundings is high; and, besides, the average length of council service of those who responded is but a few years. This seems to be additional evidence of a real, sharp decision to dissociate from council membership.

Another 9 per cent were dissuaded from membership by a belief that Councils lack significant independent powers of decision, and for that number this must be taken seriously. But the really striking feature, in a sample of this type, is that so few advanced such a view, though included in the prompt list, as a reason for their not taking part. There is no evidence – in fact, quite the contrary (Chapter 7, below) – that people of this calibre feel that Councils, including district Councils, have insufficient powers and responsibilities to make what they do significant and interesting.[1] This is true despite the emphasis laid by the sample generally upon the high importance of the work they themselves do. There was seldom a note of disparagement on this aspect of local government.

A point to which reference must be made here, though developed elsewhere (Chapter 4, below), is the statement made by eight members of the sample that their pattern of activity had developed early in other ways. In a sense all this does is to throw the point of decision further back, but it also focuses attention on the important question of *how* people enter into their commitments outside their work. Once a pattern is set up, undertakings made, relationships established, it becomes difficult to adopt a pattern of activity which is different in some fundamental ways. It is in the early years of a career that lack of time may be a truly independent

[1] Only a few appear to conclude that local government powers are fully adequate merely because of an ideological commitment to limited government.

C

factor in hindering candidacy for a Council. Many respondents, speaking generally of the problem of local government recruitment, assert that young men of the sort required are precisely those who cannot spare the time; they are developing their professional practice or expertise, or making their way up the managerial ladder under the eyes of their superiors, or, if independent, building up their business. As years go by, and their careers unfold, such people tend to move into voluntary activity within professional or business organisations. Others, who start in an established, largely inherited position, may more quickly become entangled in voluntary work. In both cases the pattern is set fairly early, and is not easily broken.

Then reference should be made to the fact that eight people mentioned financial losses as a disincentive to council membership. These are mainly direct losses of professional earnings and so forth as a consequence of attending meetings. So small a proportion is perhaps only to be expected in so wealthy a group as this,[1] though some seemed to imply that middle-class people lose more by council service since working-class people have low incomes anyway.

Finally, is there any conceivable change, either in their own circumstances or in the local government system, which respondents feel might persuade or allow them to stand as candidates for the Council? The next table sets out the replies. In general, earlier conclusions are confirmed. The top five lines taken together, with double-counting eliminated, show that well over half cannot imagine any change likely to lead to their becoming councillors. The tone of many other replies suggests that this attitude is even more widely spread amongst the

[1] Few members of the public stress financial losses either. Maud Report, III 122, table 169; p. 129, table 177.

sample. The next two lines again emphasise the time factor, and the following three lines reiterate the objections to 'politics'. The next three stress council inefficiency or reorganisation, and the two subsequent lines stress the wish to act individually not collectively, and to make one's own contribution even to a joint enterprise.

TABLE 14

Conceivable changes in personal or local government circumstances which might lead to candidature for Council

|  | No. | % |
| --- | --- | --- |
| 1. In no circumstances | 35 | 45 |
| 2. Too old now | 12 | 15 |
| 3. If retired would be too old | 7 | 9 |
| 4. Prefer other commitments | 15 | 19 |
| 5. Character, temperament unsuited; ignorant | 3 | 4 |
| 6. If retired | 17 | 22 |
| 7. If council time cut | 13 | 17 |
| 8. If no parties – as an independent | 17 | 22 |
| 9. In rural area near home | 6 | 8 |
| 10. If co-opted, or election unnecessary | 9 | 12 |
| 11. Organisation too inefficient; councillors poor; excessive bureaucracy | 9 | 12 |
| 12. If local government reorganised on regional basis | 6 | 8 |
| 13. If meetings called in evenings | 6 | 8 |
| 14. Individual work preferred | 5 | 6 |
| 15. If called; if felt could be of help; if disaster loomed | 14 | 18 |
| 16. As a change to fill in the time | 7 | 9 |
| 17. If business worry or commitment cut | 6 | 8 |

1–5: no conceivable change. 6–7: time. 8–10: politics. 11–13: reorganisation. 14–15: individualism.

# CHAPTER 4

# How and Why Notables get Involved in Voluntary Work

ANALYSIS of the notables' involvement in other voluntary work, sheds some useful light on their abstention from local council membership. First of all, Table 15 shows how they were recruited to these groups. It is rather rare that a single pattern of initiation explains the introduction of an individual to all his various activities. A man may get concerned in different voluntary tasks because of different factors. 'Family connection' may explain some activities, but 'occupation' may explain others. Still, it is possible to ascribe the participation of a majority largely to a single big factor.

The table shows that some 41 per cent stressed the

TABLE 15   Influences behind recruitment to voluntary activities

|  | No. | % |
|---|---|---|
| 1. Occupational interest | 36 | 46 |
| 2. Personal active interest | 32 | 41 |
| 3. Invited (connection) | 25 | 32 |
| 4. Approached by family, friends, colleagues | 22 | 28 |
| 5. Social obligation | 15 | 19 |
| 6. Snowballed. One thing led to another | 13 | 17 |
| 7. Family tradition | 10 | 13 |
| 8. Had useful expertise | 9 | 12 |
| 9. Accident | 7 | 9 |
| 10. Compatible colleagues attractive | 6 | 8 |

Influences behind recruitment of upper-class people
to voluntary activities

|  | % |
|---|---|
| 1. Occupational interest | 38 |
| 2. Personal active interest | 38 |
| 3. Invited (connection) | 38 |
| 4. Approached by family, friends, colleagues | 34 |
| 5. Social obligation | 13 |
| 6. Snowballed. One thing led to another | 22 |
| 7. Family tradition | 29 |
| 8. Had useful expertise | 13 |
| 9. Accident | 16 |
| 10. Compatible colleagues attractive | 9 |

Influences behind recruitment of members of
old Bristol families to voluntary activities

|  | % |
|---|---|
| 1. Occupational interest | 38 |
| 2. Personal active interest | 38 |
| 3. Invited (connection) | 28 |
| 4. Approached by family, friends, colleagues | 33 |
| 5. Social obligation | 21 |
| 6. Snowballed. One thing led to another | 21 |
| 7. Family tradition | 26 |
| 8. Had useful expertise | 10 |
| 9. Accident | 8 |
| 10. Compatible colleagues attractive | 8 |

'interest' they felt; this implies (even when they say, as
one very busy woman did, 'some people like racing,
I like this') an active, positive search to engage themselves in their chosen field, whether it be their professional organisation, education, old people's welfare and
so forth. I cannot elaborate on what aroused this
interest, but it appears often to be prompted, or sustained, by moral reflections. Thus a trade unionist asks

himself, 'Have I lived for any purpose? Is the world any better for my having lived?', whilst an industrial knight says, 'You don't like to feel you're not pulling your weight. I'm not an idle chap.' Or again, 'One feels a duty to put something back into the state – it is part of the English tradition'; and, 'One could apply one's time to making more money; it's one's duty to give some time.'

About a fifth emphasised the sense of duty to the larger city community or a particular segment of it. If these two closely related categories are combined and double-counting eliminated, rather over half the sample (54 per cent) claim to have sought positively to engage themselves in voluntary activity. If one recalls the number and variety of associations, organisations, clubs, groups, societies, offices, committees and boards with which so many of the sample concern themselves, and the hours devoted to such activity, the strength of much of the motivation is apparent. An active woman informant remarked on the relatively small numbers of participants in these affairs, as in politics: 'The same people do all these things,' she complained, 'they're a small-stage army.' The reasons for avoiding the Council are evidently a good deal more complex than they would be if we could show that most of the sample are quite passive in their involvement. It is, after all, a sociological commonplace that behaviour tends to be of a piece and a high degree of community activity is associated with considerable political involvement.

There is naturally a fairly large minority passive element. Nine per cent say their sharing in these concerns 'just happened', or developed 'by accident', largely in relation to the way in which significant acquaintance-ships were struck up. Besides, 17 per cent of the sample describe the almost autonomous way in which much of this activity can bloom – 'it snowballs', or 'one thing leads to another', as it was commonly put. Thus the commitments of about a quarter grew through the part-agency of accident, chance contact, or others' know-ledge of their incipient interests. It seems fair to comment that, in a large county borough at least, so tentative an initial commitment would only rarely lead to active council service.

Occupational factors, often in conjunction with 'duty' or 'interest' have been important in bringing nearly half into voluntary work. A further 12 per cent felt a part had been played by their possession of some profes-sional expertise in the law, or finance, or property dealing, which was of value to some voluntary body such as an independent school or welfare organisation. One may wonder at the contrasting failure of local govern-ment to associate these skills with its enterprises.

Is the *type* of voluntary activity therefore fundamen-tally important to the analysis? It might be argued that in so far as it is concerned with the well-being of a particular trade or profession, or even with industry or commerce as a whole, it cannot properly be put on all fours with council work; that, however widely inter-preted, it is too narrow and, however altruistically conceived, it is too closely related to the respondent's own economic interests to be compared with the width of interest and sympathy that impels people to serve their local authority. Only to state it like this suggests the falsity of the argument. Most occupationally or professionally inspired service has little to do with self in the narrow sense – 'one feels a duty to the trade in general; I regard myself as a representative of the trading community' – and often has wide social impli-cations in, for example, the fields of training, economic policy, planning and employment. In any case, most have at least a minor interest in some different activity, quite apart from that deriving directly from occupational cares.

Two other categories in Table 15 shed some light on our problem. Over one-quarter lay particular significance on being approached by friends, colleagues, acquaintances or family friends to join in; an additional third attribute their involvement to rather more formal invitation, from people or bodies who were aware that, for one reason or another, they might be persuaded to serve. Together, therefore, nearly two-thirds stressed personal invitation as a factor. Thus invitations to do this kind of thing were rather more common than invitations to stand for the Council, and at the same time far more sympathetically considered, though, of course, instances were given of invitations rejected. It is conceivable that more of the sample might have stood for the Council if approached in the same way, as early and as frequently as they have been by people representing other bodies; yet too much stress could be laid on this factor.

What seems to be important is the difference in the style of life typical of the council candidate and of the voluntary worker in other spheres of activity. For example, recruitment procedures to voluntary bodies, and even to public offices, like sheriff, or magistrate, are more informal and private, depending upon friendship and contact between people of similar social background, than the procedures of recruitment to local political office. This difference in style appears to be basic to understanding the problem as we shall see in Chapter 8.

In this connection the significance of the 8 per cent who mentioned the compatibility of their colleagues in voluntary groups should not be missed; in the words of one, 'I like a congenial group – I join my friends.' Moreover, a factor of some importance, mentioned by 13 per cent of the sample, was family tradition or connections leading to association with particular bodies.[1] This exceeds the proportion who can claim a recent family tradition of council service. Though nearly a quarter referred to an active interest by their forebears in local politics, very often this had terminated with the great-grandfather, grandfather or great-uncle, as the case might be. It looks as if the tradition (such as it was) of council service by the notables was already largely ended in my respondents' fathers' days, in the first two or three decades of the present century. More than one mentioned the lack of a family tradition of council service as an explanation for his not serving.

On the other hand the family tradition of voluntary service does, especially for the half of the sample hailing from established Bristol families, help to create a fairly distinctive pattern in making decisions about participating in voluntary activity.[2] The trend-setting decision is made early. Those entering upon an established position among the social notables find themselves moving, through the mediation of their friends and relatives, into membership of, and office in, a variety of institutions, often of a charitable or social nature. There is a real sense in which some of this kind

[1] An example of this type of long connection from outside the sample may be found in the *Evening Post* of 1 November 1966, which reported Mr Peter Gardner, president of the Dolphin Society, as saying that his great-great-grandfather was president of the society just over 150 years ago.

[2] The importance of the type of early 'socialisation' in the culture and sub-culture can, of course, hardly be over-emphasised. See, amongst other works, G. Almond and S. Verba, *The Civic Culture* (Princeton U.P., Princeton, N.J., 1963), passim; Rose, *Politics in England*, ch. 3; R. E. Lane, *Political Life* (Free Press of Glencoe, Chicago, 1959) pt. 4.

of activity is inherited; as one patrician said, 'I inherited a lot of comfort and I inherited this [voluntary work] too.' The pressures to accept such a state of affairs are overwhelming. The individuals concerned are young, inexperienced and flattered by the prospect; though their membership lends prestige to the institution, the latter also reflects it back on them. One socially exalted Mason said he gets treated within that society 'like royalty' – and enjoys it. The community accepts, and their own circle expects, this sort of activity; and family tradition establishes a mode of behaviour which there seems little reason to question, especially as the original objects of these institutions are very frequently eleemosynary. Such initial steps may, as we have seen, often lead to others, and over a period of years additional associations in the field, leading to an interest in, say, further education, boys' clubs, or some special aspect of welfare like the problems of old people or handicapped children may develop.

A slightly different pattern is more common amongst those of rather less patrician origin. Their movement into outside service is somewhat later and there is a slightly greater tendency to go into the more 'public' – but non-elected – kind of position, on the magistrates' bench, or hospital boards, or as income tax commissioners and the like. This progress often depends on attracting the attention of those mysterious mentors who suggest names for some sort of local book of the great and the good, and seems to be done by combining fairly high social origins with some evidence of competence. This is part of the snowball effect; one who is himself involved explained how he and fellow industrialists, often with an Oxford background, already involved in public work, enjoying contacts with the Civil Service and intimately connected with the local university, assist in suggesting names for further work of a semi-public character.

Attention will now be directed to what the sample feel about the sacrifices required by these voluntary burdens, and the compensatory satisfactions which may be earned. Views about the sacrifices appear in Table 16. Nearly half protested that there is no 'sacrifice' at all, that what is done is done dutifully or even gladly. On the other hand, a quarter, a significant minority, who do not in fact spend any more time on voluntary activities than the average of the sample as a whole, do feel quite keenly that sacrifice is involved; one even said, 'I was brought up with a sense of service, and I curse having to do it.'[1]

Such a reaction indicates that involvement by the sample is not, usually, a merely dilettante one.

TABLE 16    Sacrifices entailed by voluntary activity

|  | No. | % |
|---|---|---|
| 1. No sacrifice | 34 | 44 |
| 2. A real sacrifice | 17 | 22 |
| 3. Loss of spare time | 43 | 55 |
| 4. Private life; family suffers | 18 | 23 |
| 5. Tension; energy sapped | 8 | 10 |
| 6. Occupation suffers | 8 | 10 |
| 7. Financial losses | 8 | 10 |
| 8. Congenial friends given up | 1 | 1 |

Over half the respondents regarded the giving up of time as a sacrifice. This is a fairly obvious one, but it is very significant when it is recalled that the loss of time is also said most commonly to be the chief drawback of being a councillor (see page 54 above). Time being a limited commodity, it is clear that its consumption will

[1] The proportions of councillors who report feeling either (a) a lack of sacrifice or (b) a sacrifice quite deeply seem to resemble the proportions in my sample expressing similar feelings about their voluntary work. Maud Report, II 143.

very frequently be the most apparent cost of any item of activity upon which it may be (potentially) expended. Encroachment upon personal time by participation in these other voluntary activities is felt, but *not as an unreasonable* price, as it is for council service. The difference might be accounted for in a number of different ways; firstly, it may be felt that the amount of time taken by the Council goes over the border of toleration. This is certainly a small part of the explanation. Though their average expenditure of time on voluntary work is about as great as that by politicians on local Councils, effective council membership could possibly require a greater sacrifice by some. Another explanation might be that the particular people who object to spending time on the Council are not those individuals who are sensitive to the sacrifice of time on their own voluntary work. In fact as many as 32 of the 55 who feel that the consumption of time is a decisive obstacle to becoming a councillor also mentioned that the time given up to their voluntary work is a sacrifice, which, however, they *are willing to make*. The 38 of these 55 for whom figures are available spend, on the average, about 11 hours a week on these alternative activities. Clearly time factors as such are not adequate explanations for the difference in attitude towards council and other voluntary service, which must be related to fundamentally different assessments of their significance.

The next most commonly distinguished cost levied by voluntary activity is its effect on home and family life. About a quarter feel there are deleterious consequences upon the quality of family relationships; indeed, more than one indicated that it had contributed to family estrangements. Damaging effects within the family were not subsequently suggested as specific objections to a local government commitment, but no doubt would be subsumed within the general objection to the devotion of time to council affairs. Clearly, direct knowledge of the more or less mischievous effects that close participation in outside matters may have upon the family does not encourage expansion of such commitments by joining a Council.

Rather infrequently mentioned are sacrifices of nervous energy and peace of mind, money losses – whether due to failure to ask for expenses, to the duty to contribute, or to the neglect of business affairs – and damage to one's occupational pursuits. These are real sacrifices and not unlike those expected to be levied by council membership. The first is especially interesting; it serves to underline the point that voluntary work is no mere relaxing hobby. Of some significance to the argument developed later is the fact that only one person hinted that activity of this sort entailed giving up some contact with friends – 'one's friends don't do this sort of thing'.

Next follows (in Table 17) an analysis of the satisfactions said to be derived from voluntary work. The answers were very varied and delivered with different degrees of emphasis. Any analysis and classification must be to some extent arbitrary and distorting. Use of few categories makes the interpretation cruder by blurring some of the finer differences; use of a large number may stress differences misleadingly in so small a sample. Error in the latter direction is perhaps preferable as it does not prevent subsequent amalgamation of categories if desired.

Running through many replies is a great emphasis on achievement, on getting results, on solving problems, on being accepted, on activity leading to a desired end. With this goes a satisfaction in a very personal contribution to the results; this is implicit in a number of categories and is explicit elsewhere. 'There is some satisfaction in getting people to act along lines one has initiated': another example – 'success in contributing to the objectives of the activity – one can influence things'. Enjoying such satisfaction appears to depend, firstly, on the (oligarchic) way in which these associations tend to

TABLE 17    Satisfactions enjoyed in voluntary activity

|  | No. | % |
|---|---|---|
| 1. Creative; see results; achieve something | 24 | 31 |
| 2. Help others; service | 23 | 29 |
| 3. Meet people; stimulating | 19 | 24 |
| 4. Make a contribution; personal fulfilment | 16 | 21 |
| 5. Solving problems; intellectual | 12 | 15 |
| 6. Important; worth doing | 12 | 15 |
| 7. Broadening views; seeing others in action | 7 | 9 |
| 8. Success, kudos, doing satisfactory job | 6 | 8 |
| 9. Using power or influence | 6 | 8 |
| 10. Interest, enjoyment, satisfaction | 6 | 8 |
| 11. Continuation of business activity | 5 | 6 |
| 12. Insight into community problems | 5 | 6 |
| 13. Using one's bent or expertise | 4 | 5 |
| 14. Organising or administering | 4 | 5 |
| 15. A change | 3 | 4 |
| 16. Advance business interests | 3 | 4 |

function, and secondly, on the kind of high status that people in the sample tend to enjoy within such groups. Other satisfactions are found in helping others and in learning more about other people, their work and the community generally. Typical comments of this sort include, 'I have made a lot of friends in every walk of life', and 'One gets some broadening of horizons, insights into people and social problems – I've learned a lot and it has helped in a number of ways.' There are the satisfactions to be found in personal fulfilment, and in making use of one's knowledge, enterprise, power and abilities in a different context and on behalf of others.[1] Very few suggest that materially selfish motives are important in undertaking voluntary work. Three did, however, imply that membership of some organisations might advance one's business interests – 'Nobody joins [a voluntary body] without an eye on the main chance.' Another said, 'I came to the conclusion that there is more self than service in Rotary, so I left'; and another, 'In the professions you have to get yourself known, so there are some quid pro quos.'

The sample was next asked how it felt local council membership and other voluntary work differed in the quality of the satisfactions each offered its participants. Their replies appear in Table 18 below. It will be noticed that in the context of a direct comparison only six people held to the view that time consumption was a special drawback of being a councillor, confirming an

TABLE 18

Satisfactions of council and other voluntary work compared

|  | No. | % |
|---|---|---|
| 1. Members of both do much same sort of thing. Both make contributions | 24 | 31 |
| 2. Councillors and others serve alike – are altruistic | 4 | 5 |
| 3. Party politics in Council – opposition, axes to grind | 41 | 53 |
| 4. Council machine clumsy, impersonal, frustrating | 15 | 19 |
| 5. Poor-quality councillors | 11 | 14 |
| 6. On Council, cannot decide or get own way; need to argue | 6 | 8 |
| 7. Council claims on time excessive | 6 | 8 |
| 8. Council restricted by statute | 3 | 4 |
| 9. Council shallow, less spiritual | 2 | 3 |
| 10. Council less intensive, more diffuse in operations | 1 | 1 |

[1] The man who said, 'life overtakes you – I'm not sure that you do get satisfactions', is perhaps a clearer case than usual where the individual psychological approach could be fruitful.

Satisfactions of council and other voluntary work
compared by members of old Bristol families

| | % |
|---|---|
| 1. Members of both do much same sort of thing. Both make contributions | 23 |
| 2. Councillors and others serve alike – are altruistic | 3 |
| 3. Party politics in Council – opposition, axes to grind | 49 |
| 4. Council machine clumsy, impersonal, frustrating | 21 |
| 5. Poor-quality councillors | 23 |
| 6. On Council, cannot decide or get own way; need to argue | 10 |
| 7. Council claims on time excessive | 13 |
| 8. Council restricted by statute | 3 |
| 9. Council shallow, less spiritual | 0 |
| 10. Council less intensive, more diffuse in operations | 3 |

Satisfactions of council and other voluntary work
compared by members of upper classes

| | % |
|---|---|
| 1. Members of both do much same sort of thing. Both make contributions | 31 |
| 2. Councillors and others serve alike – are altruistic | 0 |
| 3. Party politics in Council – opposition, axes to grind | 56 |
| 4. Council machine clumsy, impersonal, frustrating | 9 |
| 5. Poor-quality councillors | 22 |
| 6. On Council, cannot decide or get own way; need to argue | 6 |
| 7. Council claims on time excessive | 3 |
| 8. Council restricted by statute | 3 |
| 9. Council shallow, less spiritual | 0 |
| 10. Council less intensive, more diffuse in operations | 3 |

earlier argument. The first two lines suggest that a third of the sample could not identify at once any significant difference between the two forms of activity in the kinds of satisfaction they give.

Other lines carry us forward in our investigations.

Well over half the respondents say that the politics in local government make a fundamental – and in their view deplorable – distinction between the style and value of council activity and other sorts of voluntary work. They say, 'It is less frustrating than political activity, which is corrupting'; or, 'there is no need of a party ideological division in local affairs'; and 'One is much freer, there is no party line, though you may have to toe a line to some extent – there are certain conventions you have to watch.' This animus against politics in local government indicates the really decisive factors shaping the pattern of their active community interests. They dislike, they say, the 'spleen' of political discussion, the 'pulling against one another', the restricted individual freedom, the frustration of being saddled with a built-in opposition, the ambitions and machines endemic in a party political system. They argue that none of this should be part of local government, and as long as it is there, then they avoid participation.

Such distaste goes beyond the rejection merely of party politics to the machinery which representative institutions hitherto, at least, have appeared to require; nearly a fifth condemn the alleged clumsiness of the system; its impersonality, the waste of time entailed by much committee work and so forth. Mingled with this is a common view that it is much more difficult to make an individual, personal contribution to the desired end, or, at least, that it is long delayed and obscured. This contrasts with the estimate of satisfactions afforded by other voluntary activities as illustrated in Table 17, and is consistent with another common opinion, that unlike council decisions, the decision-making process in 'non-political' bodies does not involve debate, discussion, opposition, conflict and argument. Yet another important difference seen by 14 per cent of the sample is that councils have too many poor-quality people on them to be attractive. Altogether, the responses tabulated in this chapter further the investigation, but more extended interpretation will wait till Chapters 8 and 9.

# CHAPTER 5

# The Notables' Contacts with, and Attitudes Towards, the Local Authority

THEIR own explanations for their behaviour can rarely be immediately accepted at their face value when the activities of any groups are being investigated. Already the evidence suggests that there are inadequacies in the somewhat *simpliste* explanations put forward by the sample to account for their roles in local politics and government. To lay some of the groundwork for a closer analysis of these roles and the values associated with them, this chapter will review the material provided by the interviews about the ideas of the sample on local representative government in general, the performance of Bristol's administration in particular, and the quality and motivation of its councillors. But first an attempt will be made to assess the degree of contact with, and knowledge of, local government enjoyed by these notables. No check has been made in council offices or with councillors and committees upon the accuracy of the testimony. It can give but a rough indication of the situation, but this seems to be all that is required.

First, in Table 19, appear the answers to an inquiry about the sources relied upon for information concerning council affairs. It is significant of the importance of the newspapers, of which we have seen they are avid readers, that nearly 90 per cent promptly mentioned the Press as a major source of information. The functions fulfilled by the Press for such people are, firstly, to give them information on developments outside their normal interests, and, secondly, to give early warning of developments in spheres where they do have particular interests – for example, preliminary discussions about the introduction of parking-meters. Generally, there is little expression of dissatisfaction with the way in which the Press carries out these functions, whatever councillors may feel.[1] The other two main points illustrated by this table are, first, the very small importance of almost any other source of information, but, second, in exception to this, the bottom six lines suggest the large part played by actual contact with personnel of the authority, whether councillors or officials, in a great variety of circumstances.

TABLE 19   Sources of information about the Council

|  | *No.* | % |
|---|---|---|
| 1. Do not follow council affairs | 5 | 6 |
| 2. Press | 68 | 87 |
| 3. T.V. | 5 | 6 |
| 4. 'Civic News' – public relations monthly sheet | 4 | 5 |
| 5. Company sources – press cuttings, official | 2 | 3 |
| 6. Chamber of Commerce | 4 | 5 |
| 7. Colleagues at work, family, etc. | 7 | 9 |
| 8. Talk about Council | 13 | 17 |
| 9. Party sources | 3 | 4 |
| 10. Councillor contacts | 29 | 37 |
| 11. Closely involved on particular problems | 24 | 31 |
| 12. Contacts with officials | 18 | 23 |
| 13. Social contacts – clubs, etc. – with councillors, etc. | 13 | 17 |
| 14. Councillors – on official occasions – as J.P.s, etc. | 11 | 14 |
| 15. Particular friends on Council | 9 | 12 |

[1] In fact some Labour councillors are rather critical.

The sample were also asked how frequently they had attended meetings, formal or informal, of the Council or its committees, and their replies are classified in Table 20. Like the general public, very few ever go to a council meeting, and the rather poor view that most entertain of the proceedings in such meetings is clearly second-hand, nearly entirely based on Press reports, almost certainly about goings-on in some neighbouring councils. But a striking difference from the experience of the general public is the contact made by about 50 per cent with committees of the Council.

TABLE 20    Attendance at council or committee meetings

|  | No. | % |
|---|---|---|
| 1. Attended neither council nor committee | 38 | 49 |
| 2. Not attended council | 29 | 37 |
| 3. Not attended committee | 2 | 3 |
| 4. Attended council | 10 | 13 |
| 5. Attended committee | 38 | 49 |
| 6. Attended Downs committee[1] | 12 | 15 |
| 7. Attended education committee | 10 | 13 |
| 8. Attended planning committee | 7 | 9 |
| 9. Attended youth committee | 3 | 4 |
| 10. Been member of Bristol Council | 5 | 6 |

So far, then, we have seen that a considerable proportion of the sample have information-yielding contacts with councillors and officials, and have been in attendance with council committee members. Table 21 below shows something of the extent of their acquaintance with councillors and officials – that is, the numbers of councillors and officials respondents say they 'know'. This can only be a rough approximation. 'A few' councillors means up to about ten; 'many' councillors

[1] A joint council and Merchant Venturers Society committee responsible for the Downs, a very large open space in the city.

means anything above this. Because there are fewer top
officials, 'many' top officials signifies anything above
four or five. The intimacy of these relationships is not
measured here, but most do not appear to be very close.
Even so, the important point is clear – that interaction
between local authority personnel and the sample is
very common.

TABLE 21
Extent of acquaintanceship with councillors and officials

|  | No. | % |
|---|---|---|
| 1. No councillors | 4 | 5 |
| 2. A few councillors | 33 | 42 |
| 3. Many councillors | 41 | 53 |
| 4. No top officials | 12 | 15 |
| 5. A few top officials | 36 | 46 |
| 6. Many top officials | 30 | 38 |

Next it was attempted to establish how often people
in the sample in the previous year had, by telephoning,
writing or visiting the Council House, sought to make
contact with councillors or officials. Table 22 shows the
sample to be divided rather evenly, with about a fifth

TABLE 22
Frequency of contacts sought with the local authority

|  | No. | % |
|---|---|---|
| 1. Nil | 18 | 23 |
| 2. Daily or weekly contact with councillor, official, or committee | 17 | 22 |
| 3. Regularly, fortnightly or monthly | 14 | 18 |
| 4. Occasionally – perhaps 8 in a year | 13 | 17 |
| 5. Rarely – quarterly or half-yearly | 13 | 17 |
| 6. Fluctuates – in waves; not now | 7 | 9 |
| 7. Social contact frequent | 6 | 8 |
| 8. Only through firm's underling | 9 | 12 |

having no such communication, and about a fifth in each other category, including that in which the individual, his group or his business are in almost constant touch. The table serves to emphasise the point made earlier – the comparatively high degree of interaction between the authority and the sample.

TABLE 23    Subjects of interaction

|  | No. | % |
|---|---|---|
| 1. Total | 58 | 100 |
| 2. Planning | 23 | 40 |
| 3. (Town Clerk) Law | 8 | 14 |
| 4. Port of Bristol Authority, Docks | 6 | 10 |
| 5. City Valuer, Estates | 4 | 7 |
| 6. Airport | 3 | 5 |
| 7. Housing | 8 | 14 |
| 8. Social work, welfare, old people, youth | 13 | 22 |
| 9. Education | 7 | 12 |
| 10. Health | 3 | 5 |
| 11. Children | 2 | 3 |
| 12. Arts, culture | 2 | 3 |
| 13. Downs | 2 | 3 |
| 14. Miscellaneous | 8 | 14 |

What will also concern us, besides the frequency and extent of this interaction, is something of the subject matter of these contacts. Why do so many members of the sample meet with local officials and councillors so frequently? Such information can help in depicting the roles played by the notables in the political system. Table 23 above shows that the matters calling for these interactions are broadly to do either and mainly with business, planning, the docks and so forth, or with welfare and cultural affairs.

The sample was further questioned about desirable methods of dealing with a problem identified in a community, about activating the local authority to deal with it, about the adequacy of their contacts with the authority and about the availability of allies they may employ to reinforce such contacts. The answers – in Table 24 – give overwhelmingly the impression that where there is a local problem it is regarded almost automatically as a responsibility of the local authority, though it should be remembered that these replies were given in the context of discussion about local government. Few appear to feel that pressure on central government pays off better, and there is little disposition towards the belief that it is unreal to approach the Council on a local matter. It is also clear that most are satisfied with the degree and quality of their intercourse with the authority. A good many of these contacts are made through subordinates; but they are usually direct, and not through intermediary bodies, though about a third mentioned some such organisation as the Chamber of Commerce or trade associates as occasional allies. It appears to be the case that a great many of these contacts are of an almost routine, businesslike character, in whose conduct few encounter obstacles. The mediation or assistance of allies is called for only in a minority of rather special cases, when, indeed, such intervention may be very valuable. A number of respondents quoted unfortunate incidents of inaccuracy or unhelpfulness on the part of the Press, but others are confident of their competence in recruiting its sympathy and active support, though this is rarely afforded in any massive way since the criterion is the Press's estimate of 'news value'.

In summary, we can see that the sample varies widely in the degree and quality of contacts experienced with the authority. For some it is very rare indeed, for others it is spasmodic, and for others yet again it is frequent and even routinised. The matters involved may be

TABLE 24   When problem arises:
(a) adequacy of council contacts, (b) allies

|  | No. | % |
|---|---|---|
| 1. Total | 63 | 100 |
| 2. Unsatisfactory contacts | 3 | 5 |
| 3. Small contacts by firm's underlings | 4 | 6 |
| 4. Minimum contact required – and had | 7 | 11 |
| 5. Little contact, but available if required | 17 | 27 |
| 6. Fair degree of adequate contact | 32 | 51 |
| 7. Press sympathetic to aims | 21 | 33 |
| 8. Trade unions sympathetic to aims | 6 | 10 |
| 9. Contact or help through Chamber of Commerce | 12 | 19 |
| 10. Contact through Bristol Council of Social Service | 3 | 5 |
| 11. Contact through Rotary | 3 | 5 |
| 12. Contact through trade associations | 3 | 5 |
| 13. Contact through influential people on same bodies | 5 | 8 |
| 14. Use *ad hoc* pressure-group | 4 | 6 |
| 15. No pressure exerted | 7 | 11 |

trivial or weighty, business affairs or welfare. Sometimes the relationship is an equal, co-operative one, at
other times the Council or the outsider may be in a
stronger or weaker position. But this section mainly
establishes the unsurpassed extent to which the local
authority is accessible to members of the sample, as well
as the variety of channels of communication open to
them.

Yet another method of assessing the sample's attitudes to participation in local council affairs is to
examine their attitudes to local representative government in general. They were asked whether a system of
electing local representatives to run local government is
a good one. The replies appear in Table 25. On the
whole it is felt that in conception the system is a good
one, and though actual practice sometimes arouses

grave doubts, it is not easy to think of a more acceptable alternative. Many feel that it is best that local problems should be dealt with by people possessed of local knowledge, and about half as many appreciate the value of local responsibility and participation. Thus, 'Yes, a safety valve; I haven't a high opinion of democracy, but it has some merits – otherwise there would be a lot of ill-feeling, and disgruntled people would form a pressure group; majority decisions have to be accepted more readily.' A medical practitioner argued that 'all progress in the Health Service has come from the periphery; there is a lack of ideas originating among Whitehall people; local initiatives is the British way of life'. About 15 per cent made suggestions hostile to the local representative system, such as 'centralise', 'hand over to officials' or 'leave it to a Town Manager'.[1] One man bluntly said he didn't believe in democracy anyway – he had been shooting in Spain, and 'everybody was happy, though poor. And what about the system in Russia, too?' Another doubted 'the value of democratic government at all levels – an advisory committee would be enough'. But this extreme view is rare. What is largely disliked about the system in practice is, first, that it is spoilt by party politics, and, second, that there are so many incompetent councillors. Those few who wish to hand the show over to the centre are exactly balanced by those who regard central intervention in local affairs as already excessive and of poor quality.[2] Generally, there is mild approval, tempered by

[1] But 43 per cent of county borough councillors would delegate more power to officials. Maud Report, II 169.

[2] In contrast, many electors in Cathcart, Glasgow, seem indifferent to the centralisation of local government. I. Budge and D. W. Urwin, *Scottish Political Behaviour* (Longmans, 1966) p. 95. But more in line with the finding here are the attitudes reported in F. Bealey and D. J. Bartholomew, 'The Local

awareness of drawbacks (as with most institutions)
in practice, offset by knowledge of even worse snags in
other systems. So far, there is no evidence of general
ideological commitment averse to the very system of
local self-government, nor any general condemnation of
the system based on experience of this or other systems.
At this level of generality the degree of alienation, or
sense of distance, from the system as a whole, seems to

TABLE 25   Attitudes to local representative government

|  | No. | % |
| --- | --- | --- |
| 1. Unqualified approval | 8 | 10 |
| 2. Approve principle, doubts in practice | 20 | 26 |
| 3. Large degree disapproval | 9 | 12 |
| 4. Dislike alternatives | 18 | 23 |
| 5. Some approval but councillors poor | 12 | 15 |
| 6. Hand over largely to centre | 7 | 9 |
| 7. Hand over to officials | 5 | 6 |
| 8. Cut functions | 6 | 8 |
| 9. Appoint and leave to Town Manager | 2 | 3 |
| 10. Spoiled by party politics | 10 | 13 |
| 11. Excessive and poor central intervention | 7 | 9 |
| 12. Want some form of regionalism | 6 | 8 |
| 13. Approve – local people know problems | 20 | 26 |
| 14. Approve – local participation, responsibility | 10 | 13 |
| 15. Approve – check on officials and centre | 4 | 5 |

be less than occurs in the rest of the population,[1] though
this type of aversion may be strong enough in, say,
10 per cent of the sample to be sufficient explanation for
their refusing to become local representatives.

As a further test of views the sample was also asked
why there is public apathy to local government, as

Elections in Newcastle under Lyme', in *British Journal of
Sociology*, XIII (1962) 354.
  [1] Maud Report, III 70; but compare p. 68, table 97.

suggested by election turn-out, and why there has been a growth in criticism of local government in recent years. These questions were very 'open-ended' and, few having reflected on the problems posed, occasional difficulties were encountered in answering. So the replies contain a wide variety of material, classified in Tables 26 and 27 below. The first five lines of Table 26 show that 37 per cent of the sample believe that apathy arises out of the feeling that elections are irrelevant because they do not decide policy, which is made either at the centre or by parties similar to each other. In the following three lines appear the explanations based upon faults in the way local government is conducted – party politics, poor-quality personnel, poor publicity – but surprisingly few respondents rely on this sort of explanation. An important group of reasons advanced by more than a third of the sample in the next six lines, suggests faults lying with the public themselves, stressing the materialism of the age and the swamping of community feeling and interest by individual selfish acquisitiveness in a sea of material possessions; 'People are too bloody well off – there is apathy everywhere.' Another 17 per cent feel that people are happy with the way things are run most of the time, but are capable of being stirred to action on the rare occasions they feel their interests to be hurt. Few respondents felt obliged to dispute the view that people are apathetic about local government, though one woman made the point that inactivity at elections does not necessarily imply apathy towards local government, and a man suggested that non-voting may be a positive act of abstention. Most explanations rest on the belief either that people find local government unimportant or faulty, or that the public themselves are fatally flawed by selfishness and individualism. Neither belief, if firmly held, could encourage active people to take part in representative government. After all, while the sample is influential on the views, or behaviour, of others, there is some reciprocity.

TABLE 26   Views on why people do not vote

|  | No. | % |
|---|---|---|
| 1. Local government unimportant | 9 | 12 |
| 2. Centre decides; local government ineffective | 12 | 15 |
| 3. Parties alike – who wins unimportant | 7 | 9 |
| 4. Voting makes little difference | 9 | 12 |
| 5. No big issues; tame; mediocre; parochial | 10 | 13 |
| 6. Dislike party politics | 5 | 6 |
| 7. Poor-quality candidates | 7 | 9 |
| 8. Poor Press publicity | 6 | 8 |
| 9. Ignorance of local government | 9 | 12 |
| 10. Apathetic; selfish; leave to others | 18 | 24 |
| 11. Materialism; lack of interest in each other | 6 | 8 |
| 12. Affluence; keeping up with Joneses | 4 | 5 |
| 13. Lazy | 4 | 5 |
| 14. Welfare State; depoliticised | 3 | 4 |
| 15. People are stirred up by issues | 4 | 5 |
| 16. People happy till hurt | 9 | 12 |
| 17. Positive abstention | 1 | 1 |

Below, in Table 27, are set out the explanations for the alleged recent growth of criticism. This time over a tenth protested that they were unaware of such a phenomenon. The first five lines comprise a group of causes critical of local government, and, in response to a question implying criticism, it is somewhat striking that so relatively few (37 per cent), put forward such explanations. Replies in the subsequent four lines make the point that party politics necessarily generate criticism. More important are the following two lines, for here half the sample resort to wide social trends to account for growing criticism – the increases in government intervention and therefore of possible points of friction with the public; and on the other hand the rise of democracy and the spread of education, bringing with them more awareness and discussion among hitherto quiescent layers of the population. Nearly one-third see these latter factors as lying behind criticism of the local government system.

TABLE 27    Views on why people criticise local government

|  | No. | % |
|---|---|---|
| 1. Dislike party politics | 9 | 12 |
| 2. Poor communications with the public | 5 | 6 |
| 3. Poor-quality councillors | 9 | 12 |
| 4. Controversial issues | 5 | 6 |
| 5. Inefficiency; cumbrous procedures | 7 | 9 |
| 6. Party politics entails criticism | 4 | 5 |
| 7. Representative – in public eye | 3 | 4 |
| 8. Conflicting wants; an obvious Aunt Sally | 9 | 12 |
| 9. Interest groups; loud minority; disappointed clientele | 6 | 8 |
| 10. More contact; more government intervention | 16 | 21 |
| 11. More education; levelling; awareness; discussion | 23 | 29 |
| 12. Dislike paying rates | 7 | 9 |
| 13. Press sensationalism | 4 | 5 |
| 14. Trivia attacked; good work ignored | 5 | 6 |
| 15. Unaware of greater criticism | 9 | 12 |

Whatever the objective accuracy of the replies set out in these two tables, they have some significance here. They show a fairly widespread acceptance among the sample of a belief that many members of the public disparage elections and regard local government as unimportant or faulty; they show sensitivity to the fact that the representative system inevitably involves discussion and conflict; they indicate consciousness of social trends which have led to greater government intervention and to more social and political equality, which is expressed, by people formerly inferior in these respects, either by a selfish bent for material acquisitions, or by discussion and criticism of government, its policies and its personnel. Thus, while deep ideological or pragmatic commitment against local representative government appears to be almost absent from the sample, the framework of opinion and of social trends within which it is felt to be set are not such as to encourage participation by the sorts of people represented in the sample.

Other questions asked of the sample were designed to provide information enabling some measure to be made of their practical knowledge of the work and problems of local government in Bristol, and to gauge further the depth and reality of their interest in matters of local concern. On one level, if interest were negligible, there would be little point in pursuing the original objective of the investigation; at another level, any information on these lines would help to fill out our picture of the roles of members of the sample in the political system. Then, too, their views on the standard of performance of the Council in coping with its duties might, if either particularly negative or very favourable, provide clues as to the cause of their abstention from participation. Another probe was made into views about the relevance of local government to the problems identified as facing this community, in order to measure their estimate of the importance of council work. Subsequently there will be some discussion of replies to an inquiry about deficiencies in the local administration to see if there may be particular areas of alleged inferior performance which put the whole of Bristol's local government in a poor light.

A general evaluation of the Corporation's success in tackling its work, accompanied by some specific criticisms, appears in Table 28; seven people gave no useful answer. There were comments, which are not included, by two or three in each case, on the docks, housing, traffic, police, welfare, the airport and so forth. On the whole, the verdict is a favourable one – 'they got their priorities right after the war, and have stuck to their policies'. In holding this view, they seem to resemble the general public.[1] Assessment of the Corporation's performance as 'average' is rarely in comparison with other local authorities, which most members of the sample feel to be generally worse than Bristol, but rather in comparison with some vague standard of an administrative system, or with an idealised picture drawn from business or professional experience. In arriving at this evaluation they made many references to various incidents or features in the work of different departments. More general criticisms of the quality of the system were made – 'lack of imagination'; 'both parties promise more than they can carry out'; 'if councillors override officials they nearly always go wrong'; 'local government is too windy – like the Chamber of Commerce'. The evil effects of 'politics' were mentioned again by over a quarter, and while a fifth were able to praise the competence of officials none suggested that good qualities in councillors contributed to their reasonably favourable verdict on Bristol's government.[2] These views are based on the relative

[1] Maud Report, III 63–4.

[2] For the rise of professional officials to the eminence of 'public persons' in Cheshire County government, see Lee, *Social Leaders*, pp. 104–56. Despite the respect for them felt by part of the sample, it is doubtful if Bristol's officials' status or roles have developed to quite such a degree, probably in part due to the strong party system. See also Newcastle under Lyme where policy is not in the hands of the officials; Bealey, *et al.*, *Constituency Politics*, p. 407.

absence of any recent obvious disasters or blunders; on efficient service in routine matters; on successes to offset against failures; and on appreciation of official competence and of the policy limitations and financial stringency largely imposed by the central government. Clearly the nature of this verdict on Bristol's civic accomplishment cannot explain why the members of this sample choose not to take part. It is neither so bad that it could be argued that we should have nothing to do with so incompetent a band of rogues, nor so good that the notables could feel there was no scope for them to make a useful contribution.

TABLE 28    Views on the running of Bristol's city government

|  | *No.* | % |
|---|---|---|
| 1. Very well run; much above average | 10 | 13 |
| 2. Well run; above average | 11 | 14 |
| 3. Fairly well run; average | 42 | 54 |
| 4. Not well run; not impressed | 6 | 8 |
| 5. Politics causes changes and bad decisions | 21 | 27 |
| 6. Hindered by central or financial limits | 9 | 12 |
| 7. Delay, red tape, bureaucracy, distance from people | 13 | 17 |
| 8. Poor-quality councillors | 12 | 15 |
| 9. Not all officials of good quality | 8 | 10 |
| 10. Officials competent | 15 | 19 |
| 11. Officials need more power | 7 | 9 |
| 12. Parochial, out-of-date, unimaginative | 10 | 13 |
| 13. Education provision good | 11 | 14 |
| 14. Education policy and implementation – disagree | 20 | 26 |
| 15. Planning good | 6 | 8 |
| 16. Planning poor | 21 | 27 |

They were then asked to suggest the problems that might face the city in the next decade or so. The object was partly to gauge the extent of their knowledge and interest, and partly to establish the context for asking

D

how relevant they feel local government to be to the solution of problems so identified. Table 29 shows the results. Once more there is little tendency to minimise the importance of local government in relation to a series of most important problems. Few suggested that these do not merit the attention of the most prominent of local notables. Doubts about the competence of councillors provide the basis of most fears about the adequacy of the municipal corporation to fulfil its role, but even these are voiced by only a small minority. Amongst the problems picked out, education, a very live issue locally, is clearly important, but is overshadowed by the complex of questions connected with the expected rapid growth of Bristol in population and industry, due not only to over-all national trends, but also to the improvement of communications with the crossing of the north–south M5 and the east–west M4 near by, and the opening up of South Wales and the Severn basin with the completion of the Severn bridge. Together with the city's official recognition as a regional capital in the new scheme of regional planning, with its traditional stable, varied and modestly prosperous industrial base, and high hopes of intensive port-development, this has given rise to expectations of large expansion here in the next ten or twenty years.[1] A very high proportion of the sample made usually favourable reference to such developments and to associated problems of housing, communication, planning and welfare. Few (mainly clergymen) identify more basic social problems and, for example, only a handful see race antagonisms as a difficulty, even when promp-

[1] Bristol is on her way to regaining her position as second city in the land according to the president of the Bristol Auctioneers and Estate Agents Association (Bristol) *Evening Post*, 23 Nov 1967).

ted. More are perturbed by signs of growing control from London in both the public and the private spheres; according to an ex-county and rural district councillor, 'Nothing said in the Town Hall or County Hall has any effect; the officials just interpret Whitehall policy'. Others say local authorities are too local in character. Any feelings that problems of distributive justice remain for solution did not rise to the surface. The small handful concerned about slum housing conditions are offset by those criticising the provision of housing for better-off people.

TABLE 29   Problems likely to face Bristol
in the next 10–20 years

| | No. | % |
|---|---|---|
| 1. Local government highly relevant | 33 | 42 |
| 2. Local government relevant | 23 | 30 |
| 3. Local government fairly relevant | 15 | 19 |
| 4. Local government not relevant | 3 | 4 |
| 5. Local government relevant but councillors inadequate | 9 | 12 |
| 6. Immigration a problem | 6 | 8 |
| 7. Education reorganisation and politics | 18 | 23 |
| 8. Breakdown of community, of family | 5 | 6 |
| 9. Housing | 21 | 27 |
| 10. Growth of city; industry; port expansion; region | 34 | 44 |
| 11. Roads, traffic, air communications, Portbury | 34 | 44 |
| 12. Lack of planning, and planning failures | 15 | 19 |
| 13. Planning | 13 | 17 |
| 14. Lack of money | 6 | 8 |
| 15. Growth of control by London | 8 | 10 |
| 16. Too local an organisation | 8 | 10 |

Table 30 confirms the picture already emerging by showing the responses to questions about what the sample feel to be current inadequacies in local government's care for the community. Nearly one-half the sample found it either impossible or very difficult to mention any concrete instances of inadequacy. No one sphere of policy, department or committee comes in for an outstanding degree of criticism. Taking together the second and third lines, about one-third mention planning or traffic problems, but this is hardly excessive in view of the extreme visibility of planning mistakes (of which there are notable examples), the impact of planning policy on the convenience and aesthetics of the environment, and the especially close business concern of many of the sample with planning and traffic matters. Replies then tail off in a manner perhaps to be expected of people suddenly asked to supply evidence of deficiencies when on the whole they are reasonably satisfied with the general performance of the authority.[1]

TABLE 30    Inadequacies in Bristol's municipal policies

|  | No. | % |
|---|---|---|
| 1. Little or no inadequacy | 37 | 47 |
| 2. Planning | 16 | 21 |
| 3. Traffic, roads and parking | 13 | 17 |
| 4. Education policy implementation | 12 | 15 |
| 5. Race relations | 9 | 12 |
| 6. Parochial, not promotional | 8 | 10 |
| 7. Housing | 7 | 9 |
| 8. Arts, culture | 7 | 9 |
| 9. Provision for the old | 6 | 8 |
| 10. Wrong priorities | 3 | 4 |
| 11. Neglect voluntary bodies | 2 | 3 |
| 12. Care for youth | 2 | 3 |
| 13. Slum clearance | 2 | 3 |
| 14. Health | 2 | 3 |
| 15. Destruction of old city | 1 | 1 |

[1] Urban councillors, too, are concerned about planning and traffic, but much more so about housing than this sample. Maud Report, II 116–17.

In summary, therefore, one could say that while a few criticise the Corporation most bitterly on general grounds, and a few are ready to criticise particular areas of policy most severely, the majority are at least mildly favourable to the over-all performance of the authority, whilst singling out particular sectors for special praise or blame. Planning and education arouse most passion; while a Conservative, discussing the Labour Council's comprehensivisation policy, said, 'I rather agree on schools policy – they thought it out pretty carefully and came to the right decision', a member of the university council felt that 'education is exceedingly inefficient; there is a lack of effectiveness and the things taught are irrelevant for after life'. However, the problems seen to be facing the community now and in the future cover an even wider spectrum of affairs, and yet to their solution the great majority think local government relevant or even highly so. Confessing that as a true conservative he preferred the *status quo*, one man – 'lacking', he says, 'the zeal of a reformer' – believes that 'the less local government interferes the better'. But he is very isolated in so extreme a view. As a whole the sample appears to recognise the importance, relevance and success of Bristol's government in as great if not in greater measure than they believe the rest of the community are prepared to do.

Finally, an attempt is made here to explore views about the councillors rather than the system – about their competence and motivations, about their 'style' as councillors, about their merits and demerits, and about the kind of person preferred to serve on local authorities. Table 31 shows the unprompted views of the sample as to why councillors seek to become councillors, and Table 32 shows any fresh answers to the same inquiry after prompting by a list of six possible factors;

*entries in Table 32 are wholly additional to entries in Table 31.*

TABLE 31    Views of motivation in becoming
a council member – unprompted

|  | No. | % |
|---|---|---|
| 1. To serve the community – altruism | 66 | 85 |
| 2. Ego satisfied – self-importance | 35 | 45 |
| 3. To exercise power or influence | 18 | 23 |
| 4. To improve own status | 16 | 21 |
| 5. Interest; enjoy way of life; politics | 12 | 15 |
| 6. To help their business | 11 | 14 |
| 7. To further a political career | 9 | 12 |
| 8. Unsuccess in business or other occupation | 7 | 9 |
| 9. Part of a trade union career | 6 | 8 |
| 10. Outlet to achieve things | 6 | 8 |
| 11. To compensate for own frustrations | 6 | 8 |
| 12. Fills in time for the retired | 4 | 5 |
| 13. Been pressured into standing | 4 | 5 |
| 14. To put an idea across; an ideology; bee in bonnet | 4 | 5 |
| 15. Poor types; small men | 3 | 4 |

TABLE 32    Views of motivation in becoming
a council member – prompted

|  | No. | % |
|---|---|---|
| 1. To get an interesting outlet for energies | 41 | 53 |
| 2. To improve own status | 37 | 47 |
| 3. To compensate for frustrations | 29 | 37 |
| 4. To get promotion at work | 8 | 10 |
| 5. To help the community | 8 | 10 |
| 6. To make money | 4 | 5 |

Most respondents made the point, firstly, that motivations are usually mixed and, secondly, that different individuals are differently motivated. Some protested that they could only guess, but most gave their views quite happily. Both tables show that few believe that crude material gain is at all a common motive. Indeed, when prompted, most denied this to be the case, especially in Bristol; many feel that the reverse is true, that people lose money or promotion by council service.

Table 32 demonstrates that the great majority of the sample believe spontaneously that at least a considerable proportion of Bristol's councillors are largely motivated by an altruistic desire to serve their community in some way. This proportion rises to 95 per cent, when are added those who assented to the view when put to them. Even allowing for the conventional need to speak well of others, especially to strangers, this looks like a remarkable tribute to the character of Bristol's councillors. Few respondents left it there, however, and both tables show the great importance attached to other motives. I have attempted to distinguish between a drive for higher (objective) status and a desire for increased self-esteem, though few of the sample made this distinction explicit. But a good deal of emphasis is put on vanity, and altogether nearly 90 per cent believe, prompted or unprompted, that the drive for these twin goals is important. It is therefore roughly equivalent to the degree of belief in altruism as a factor.

Another milder type of ego-gratification, satisfying an interest or finding an outlet for energies, was put forward without prompting by a few, but over half accepted this rather vague formulation when put to them. Perhaps fairly closely allied to it is the view entertained by nearly half the sample that council service is often a compensation for disappointing frustrations at home or at work. Some recognise that there are men on the Labour side who might well feel frustrated by their low status at work and seek to get recognition in another sphere, the Council.[1] In addition, some believe that a number of people are on the Council because they are relative failures, or are uninterested in their business. As more than one said, 'One asks, why do they have the time to do this?', mainly with reference to the small businessmen on the Citizen benches. On the other hand, though one or two confessed to guilt feelings about their own non-participation on the Council, most do not see it as in some sense a 'failure'; rather it is a tribute to their occupational success.

A quarter of the sample see the search for power and influence as an important motivation. An air of disapproval attached to this, yet it will be recalled that only two respondents, even when prompted, ascribed their own reluctance to become council members even partially to a reluctance to wield power. But apparently the perception of council membership as associated with the use of power is not foreign where others are concerned. Together with other categories in Table 31, it seems that beliefs that councillors are attracted by power, by a political way of life, by furthering a political or trade union career, and by the prospect of putting across ideas to others, all build up a view of council membership as involving a special style of activity, a way of life of its own. Some 41 per cent appear to express such a view. Taken with other evidence pointing in the same direction this may be a significant indication of causes of non-participation by our economic and social notables and will be considered later.

The sample was next asked for opinions on why most councillors wish to remain councillors. In Table 33 the

[1] Manual working-class councillors corroborate this view; Maud Report, II 146, 150. See also Birch, *Small-Town Politics*, p. 115.

view is especially prevalent that councillors belong to a special group, pursuing their own way of life, being and behaving apart from others. The notion of serving the community is seen as much less usual a reason for remaining a councillor than for becoming one. Instead, 'interest', 'the exercise of power', 'receiving deference', 'a feeling of self-importance', 'being caught up in a way of life', 'belonging to an in-group', 'achieving political ambitions', are all felt to be important by sizeable sections of the sample, and all of them demonstrate awareness of the Council as being a special social group with shared norms, goals and modes of behaviour peculiar to it.

TABLE 33    Why councillors remain on the Council

|  | No. | % |
|---|---|---|
| 1. Sense of achievement; serving the public | 25 | 32 |
| 2. Interest, outlet; use of a specialism | 23 | 29 |
| 3. Sense of power, of influencing others | 18 | 23 |
| 4. Have status, respect, deference, social elevation | 17 | 22 |
| 5. Self-importance, self-glory, pomp, egotism | 16 | 21 |
| 6. Club-like social side; meeting people | 10 | 13 |
| 7. Caught up in a way of life, widens views | 9 | 12 |
| 8. Being in an in-group; at heart of things; seeing wheels turn | 8 | 10 |
| 9. Cut and thrust of debate; argument; being a politician | 8 | 10 |
| 10. Ambition; Lord Mayor's baton; political advance | 2 | 3 |

Earlier we have seen something of what the sample thinks about representative government, about Bristol's municipal administration and about the motivations of the city's councillors; now Table 34 shows their assessments of what sort of people they are who sit on the city Council. It is apparent that their personal characteristics, while acknowledged to be varied and mixed, are assessed

D 2

on the whole less highly than their motivations for joining the Council. As the first three lines show, some feel that the composition of the Council contains a good and acceptable cross-section of the community; another small group emphasises the honesty and benevolence of the generality of our councillors; and yet a third group enthuses about the capacities and qualities of some councillors. But only about a third of the sample are so favourable. Nearly as many condemn councillors as but 'a second eleven', as not being chosen out of the 'Top 250 people of the community', or even as 'damn poor'. Small groups deprecate the Council more specifically as containing too many councillors who are small and not very successful businessmen, or who are too old or too parochial and lacking width of experience, depth of education and intellectual capacity. All in all, many concede that motivation in becoming a councillor is reasonably creditable, but believe that as members

TABLE 34   Views of the quality of Bristol councillors

|  | No. | % |
|---|---|---|
| 1. Good cross-section; reasonable | 12 | 15 |
| 2. Honest, well-meaning, altruistic | 10 | 13 |
| 3. Some very good – in education, capacity, character | 11 | 14 |
| 4. Very varied | 13 | 17 |
| 5. Mediocre; damn poor | 24 | 31 |
| 6. Many inferior businessmen | 11 | 15 |
| 7. Parochial; lack width of knowledge; experience | 8 | 10 |
| 8. Too few top business or professional people | 13 | 17 |
| 9. Low intellectual level | 9 | 12 |
| 10. Lack education | 8 | 10 |
| 11. Too old | 10 | 13 |
| 12. Too prejudiced; chips on shoulders | 6 | 8 |
| 13. Trade unionists | 4 | 5 |
| 14. Dominated by officers | 2 | 3 |
| 15. Like to hear own voices | 2 | 3 |

become part of the system such motivation tends to weaken, and that in any case the capacities and experience of many councillors do not measure up to the standard most of the sample would like to establish.

Table 35 indicates the sort of people they would like to see serving on the Council. A fairly unambiguous pattern is apparent. A good deal of value is attached to the Council being a good 'cross-section', but nearly twice as many feel we lack this as feel we already enjoy it. They mean by 'a good cross-section' not a mirror proportional representation of social classes but a representation of groups so defined by themselves, usually professional and business groups, that it would *increase* the existing bias to the middle class. There is a common lack of sensitivity to the fact that some 70 per cent of the national population belong to the manual working-class.[1] One or two actually asked for a greater representation of the 'middle class', as the repository of educated ability. But the most usual point to make – by nearly half the sample – was the need of more of the city's top business notables, with their proved experience and competence, to raise the quality of council membership. True, 'high-quality people are already busy' and 'the best industrial brains have no time', but a handful of names, the same handful, was frequently mentioned, and most are in fact included in the sample. 'If some of —— ——'s knowledge and ability were applied to local government we should all benefit.' Others also stressed the potential contribution of leading professional people: 'We want a high standard of rectitude, a sense of responsibility, which tends to exist in the professional classes more than in others.' Yet others advocated the participation of the community's

[1] Councillors are often unaware of the inadequacies in local representation; Maud Report, II 83, table 2.38.

TABLE 35  The sort of council members to be preferred

|  | No. | % |
|---|---|---|
| 1. Cross-section much as it is | 10 | 13 |
| 2. Cross-section now lacking | 17 | 22 |
| 3. Top business leaders of proved experience and ability | 35 | 45 |
| 4. Professional people | 12 | 15 |
| 5. Natural leaders; people of standing in their occupation | 9 | 12 |
| 6. Experts; people with special knowledge | 7 | 9 |
| 7. Educated people | 9 | 12 |
| 8. People of intelligence and judgement | 14 | 18 |
| 9. Academics, intellectuals | 6 | 8 |
| 10. People with social conscience, desiring to serve community | 4 | 5 |
| 11. People of integrity, with values | 7 | 9 |
| 12. Unbiased people; non-party independents | 11 | 14 |
| 13. Younger people | 5 | 6 |
| 14. More housewives | 3 | 4 |
| 15. More middle class | 3 | 4 |

Views of old Bristol family members

|  | % |
|---|---|
| 1. Cross-section much as it is | 13 |
| 2. Cross-section now lacking | 21 |
| 3. Top business leaders of proved experience and ability | 46 |
| 4. Professional people | 10 |
| 5. Natural leaders; people of standing in their occupation | 10 |
| 6. Experts; people with special knowledge | 8 |
| 7. Educated people | 13 |
| 8. People of intelligence and judgement | 18 |
| 9. Academics, intellectuals | 3 |
| 10. People with social conscience, desiring to serve community | 3 |
| 11. People of integrity, with values | 8 |
| 12. Unbiased people; non-party independents | 18 |
| 13. Younger people | 5 |
| 14. More housewives | 3 |
| 15. More middle class | 0 |

'natural leaders' or those who had demonstrated their qualities at the top of their occupational ladders. Intelligence, expertise, education, success are all felt to be desirable in our councillors, though education as such is rarely regarded as the fundamental desideratum. Most urge the desirability of experience and competence, to be found at the head of any occupation, but mostly assumed to be present in greatest degree in top businessmen and professionals.

CHAPTER 6

# The Relationship of the Notables to the Local Political Structure

PREVIOUS chapters have described the responses of the sample to the questions put to them about their voluntary activities, their attitudes to local government and to service upon the Council. The true significance of their replies can, however, only be properly appreciated when the roles played by members of the sample in the political system are more exactly delineated and taken into account. The remaining chapters will seek to explain the pattern of their political behaviour, which includes their absence from the Council, by interpreting the evidence presented in the interviews in the light of some of the relationships between these people and the rest of local society, and also between them and the local government structure.

Participation and non-participation in politics, like other behaviour, can often in part be satisfactorily explained, or at least illuminated, by reference to individual psychological needs,[1] which will not, however, be attempted here. Instead, explanation will be in terms of social needs which are met by the sorts of participation typical of the group as a whole. The validity of the explanation will depend therefore to some extent on the

[1] For example, R. E. Lane, *Political Life*, chs 9, 10, 11 and *Political Ideology* (Free Press of Glencoe, Chicago, 1962).

degree to which it is correct to view the sample as representative of a group within society, rather than merely as individuals bracketed together in a statistical category.

Various grounds for considering them as such have already been adduced in Chapter 2. It will be recalled that half the sample can be described as belonging to established front-ranking Bristol families; the rest are immigrants or have sprung from more obscure origins. This division, suggestive in some respects, is, however, largely overlaid by the fact that most of the second group, always excluding the two trade union officials, share the values and way of life of the first. For example, at eleven hours a week the average time spent on voluntary activities by members of established Bristol families is exactly the same as that spent by the whole sample. Moreover, the attitudes of the sample as a whole are echoed in uncannily precise terms by these sub-groups. Table 35 indicates the close similarity of views held by the whole sample and by members of old Bristol families about the sort of council members they prefer; similarly Table 15 shows the agreement between the sample as a whole, upper-class members of the sample and members of old Bristol families in their estimates of the sorts of influences important in recruiting them to voluntary activities; again, Table 18 exhibits the close correspondence in the assessments made by the same groups of the relative satisfactions to be gained from participation in council and other voluntary work. The point is repeated in Tables 36 and 37 below, which show that though members of the old Bristol families, members of the professions and members of the upper middle and middle classes each differ in detail in interesting but not unaccountable ways from the views of other notables in their reasons for not joining

the Council, the parallels are far more striking. And
it should be remembered that the sample as a whole, and
these special groups, all differ in the *same* ways from a
*national* sample; for instance, in the stress they lay upon
their dislike of various aspects of 'politics'.

They have similarly high economic and social positions in the community and often belong to the same
associations. There were men from both categories in
the company seeking a local radio franchise before the
Government announced its policy for local radio. The
sample included 6 of the 23 associates in the Harlech
Consortium subsequently set up to bid successfully for
the local Wales and West commercial television rights,
and these, too, included members of both new and old

TABLE 36   Reasons given by whole sample of 78
for not seeking to become a council member

|  | No. | % |
|---|---|---|
| 1. Excessive calls on time | 55 | 71 |
| 2. Other activities preferred | 33 | 42 |
| 3. Dislike close party attachment and discipline | 30 | 38 |
| 4. Dislike party politics in local government | 23 | 29 |
| 5. Business comes first | 20 | 26 |
| 6. Dislike elections | 20 | 26 |
| 7. Work or positions requires non-partisan appearance | 19 | 24 |
| 8. Awkward times of meetings | 19 | 24 |
| 9. Poor quality of councillors | 18 | 23 |
| 10. Doubts on personal suitability | 16 | 21 |
| 11. Cumbrous machine | 11 | 14 |
| 12. Job needs not predictable | 10 | 13 |
| 13. Frustration by inefficiency | 9 | 12 |
| 14. Different pattern of activity developed | 8 | 10 |
| 15. Not sufficiently individual | 8 | 10 |
| 16. Dislike of publicity | 8 | 10 |
| 17. Was not invited | 7 | 9 |
| 18. Council lacks power | 7 | 9 |

## Reasons given by 39 members of old Bristol families

| | % |
|---|---|
| 1. Excessive calls on time | 69 |
| 2. Other activities preferred | 44 |
| 3. Dislike close party attachment and discipline | 38 |
| 4. Dislike party politics in local government | 31 |
| 5. Business comes first | 26 |
| 6. Dislike elections | 28 |
| 7. Work or positions requires non-partisan appearance | 18 |
| 8. Awkward times of meetings | 15 |
| 9. Poor quality of councillors | 28 |
| 10. Doubts on personal suitability | 21 |
| 11. Cumbrous machine | 13 |
| 12. Job needs not predictable | 8 |
| 13. Frustration by inefficiency | 15 |
| 14. Different pattern of activity developed | 8 |
| 15. Not sufficiently individual | 18 |
| 16. Dislike of publicity | 13 |
| 17. Was not invited | 5 |
| 18. Council lacks power | 8 |

## Reasons given by the 32 members of the upper and upper middle classes

| | % |
|---|---|
| 1. Excessive calls on time | 72 |
| 2. Other activities preferred | 47 |
| 3. Dislike close party attachment and discipline | 34 |
| 4. Dislike party politics in local government | 29 |
| 5. Business comes first | 34 |
| 6. Dislike elections | 41 |
| 7. Work or positions requires non-partisan appearance | 16 |
| 8. Awkward times of meetings | 22 |
| 9. Poor quality of councillors | 29 |
| 10. Doubts on personal suitability | 22 |
| 11. Cumbrous machine | 19 |
| 12. Job needs not predictable | 15 |
| 13. Frustration by inefficiency | 6 |
| 14. Different pattern of activity developed | 13 |
| 15. Not sufficiently individual | 13 |
| 16. Dislike of publicity | 2 |
| 17. Was not invited | 9 |
| 18. Council lacks power | 13 |

#### Reasons given by 26 members of the professions

|  | % |
|---|---|
| 1. Excessive calls on time | 88 |
| 2. Other activities preferred | 38 |
| 3. Dislike close party attachment and discipline | 46 |
| 4. Dislike party politics in local government | 23 |
| 5. Business comes first | 23 |
| 6. Dislike elections | 23 |
| 7. Work or positions requires non-partisan appearance | 31 |
| 8. Awkward times of meetings | 38 |
| 9. Poor quality of councillors | 15 |
| 10. Doubts on personal suitability | 15 |
| 11. Cumbrous machine | 8 |
| 12. Job needs not predictable | 8 |
| 13. Frustration by inefficiency | 8 |
| 14. Different pattern of activity developed | 8 |
| 15. Not sufficiently individual | 4 |
| 16. Dislike of publicity | 12 |
| 17. Was not invited | 8 |
| 18. Council lacks power | 8 |

TABLE 37

Consideration given by whole sample to going on Council

|  | No. | % |
|---|---|---|
| 1. Not thought of it seriously | 57 | 73 |
| 2. Thought of it, but decided against | 13 | 17 |
| 3. Thought of it, and joined a Council | 8 | 10 |

Consideration given to going on Council by members
of old Bristol families

|  | % |
|---|---|
| 1. Not thought of it seriously | 69 |
| 2. Thought of it, but decided against | 18 |
| 3. Thought of it, and joined a Council | 13 |

Consideration given to going on Council by members
of the upper and upper middle classes

| | % |
|---|---|
| 1. Not thought of it seriously | 72 |
| 2. Thought of it, but decided against | 16 |
| 3. Thought of it, and joined a Council | 13 |

Consideration given to going on Council
by members of the professions

| | % |
|---|---|
| 1. Not thought of it seriously | 73 |
| 2. Thought of it, but decided against | 19 |
| 3. Thought of it, and joined a Council | 8 |

families. There are often close personal and social relationships between members of the sample; according to one informant 'all the prominent businessmen live outside Bristol and know each other – they can't disentangle their business and private lives'. Another example of close and equal relations is afforded by the minister and his congregation, for the sample includes clergymen and members of their flocks, well known to them. Other professional men may be even more intimately involved. Nearly all these people have by now lived for long periods in this style within the area. While there is no formal, institutional structure to the group as such, the great majority share such informal links.[1]

That the sample is representative of a group possessing common bonds may be admitted, but it must be shown also that these relationships within the group

[1] Relationships between upper-class 'neighbours' around Banbury seem fairly comparable, but are perhaps more exclusive; Stacey, *Tradition and Change*, pp. 144–5, 151, 154.

differ to some extent from relationships between group members and the rest of society. There is not a lot of difficulty in doing this. It has already been mentioned that assistance was given in selecting the sample by men and women to whom it made sense to distinguish between 'influential' and other people; moreover, they often agreed in their particular selections. Whatever 'influential' means precisely, it implies an important difference between the relations of 'influential' people with the rest of society, and the relations enjoyed by others with society. Their almost exclusively 'upper-middle'- and 'middle'-class character is a further distinguishing feature of the group. The positions of authority in business, the professions and voluntary associations, occupied by individual members of the group; the wealth and comfort of the vast majority – these things, too, mark them off from most other members of society, and contribute to give them a special status, associated with deference and respect from others.[1] Where there is no formal structure and no clear boundaries, no formal rules of membership nor methods of enrolment, no collective action for common goals and no distinguishing marks like shared physical peculiarities, it is unlikely that a group can be quite clearly differentiated from the rest of society. That is the position of the group under discussion, but it is evident that most of the individuals within it share some characteristics and patterns of relationships not shared outside the group.

Not only do these individuals have much in common

[1] For a discussion of studies in local status systems see D. E. G. Plowman, W. E. Minchinton and Margaret Stacey 'Local Social Status in England and Wales', in *Sociological Review*, N.S., x (1962) 161–72. They comment on the difficulty of delineating a social-status system in a large population (p. 163).

which is not shared with other elements in society, but the place they occupy within the general social framework is a special one. Without entering here into the problem of whether the shape of our society should be pictured as a more or less pointed pyramid, or as a truncated one, or as one with multiple apexes, it is rather clear that our group occupies a superior rather than an inferior position. Although the term 'notables' has been preferred, if there is any truth in the 'élite' concept, and if Bristol has an élite, then the sample is largely representative of it. In one sense of the term, they are indeed members of élites – that is, they are successful leaders in their occupational spheres. They are at or near the summits of whatever occupational ladders they stand upon, locally, regionally or even nationally. They are aware of it too; one professional woman discussing the source of her influence said her grade was at the 'top' of her profession, and speaking of others like her said 'they've got something about them to have got to the top'. Other practitioners of the same arts, other members of the same social class, acknowledge their leadership, respect their opinions and judgement. Many of them are people to whom others turn precisely for their expertise or experience. Others are recognised, less precisely, as business leaders, as heads of successful business enterprises. It seems not unreasonable to conclude that, in this sense of the term, the members of the sample do belong to élites.[1]

It is less easy to demonstrate that they comprise an

---

[1] Cf. T. B. Bottomore, *Élites and Society* (Penguin, 1966) pp. 14, 77–82. D. C. Miller seems to be correct in failing to find a single 'solidary élite' in Bristol, whilst emphasising the strength of the links within the business leadership (*American Journal of Sociology*, LXIV 309). On the complexity of the make-up of the élite, see Rose, *Politics in England*, pp. 110–17.

élite in the sense popularised by Mosca and Pareto – as a cohesive group with a specially close relationship to the political power-holders in our society. Some analysis of what these relations are will be attempted below. But the proposition is not easy to demonstrate mainly because it is not at all clear whether such a group does exist in the fullest sense. However, in so far as the theory rests upon the analysis of society into ruling and non-ruling elements it looks as if the sample represents part, at least, of the ruling groups. If there is an élite in this sense, it is difficult to understand whom it could contain if it excluded these people. It is not inconsistent with this view of the nature of the élite that the group includes members sufficiently peripheral to it to act as links with the non-élite.

We do not have to rely on élitist theory to establish the strong presumption that the sample represents people who enjoy superior positions within the social structure. Their social-class background suggests the same thing. Tables 1 and 2 have shown the overwhelmingly upper- and middle-class nature of the sample. Whatever difficulties surround the concept of élites, and, indeed, whatever problems are posed by social-class theories, most people would agree that England is in some sense a class society, connoting positions of relative superiority and inferiority. Our conclusion with the aid of élite and class hypotheses that the sample are in the superior strata rather than the inferior ones, is buttressed by the fact of their occupation of objective positions of authority at work and in other types of organisation. Doubt may be felt about the reliability of élite or class concepts as guides, but members of the sample hold ample authority over others in the possession of concrete positions of power in specific organisations. They enjoy high status, even if the deference they receive is today somewhat attenuated.[1] The employee of the large industrial corporation, or the ordinary member of the British Legion branch, can be in no doubt of the authority of the chairmen of either of these two institutions, and it is with such people that we are concerned.

Moreover, members of the sample see themselves not as ordinary constituents of society but as having special, superior places within it, with shared bonds, even if none used the expression 'élite' himself. Speaking of patterns of residence, one man quite unthinkingly referred to him and his like as 'top people'. Another consciously groped for the word 'patrician' to describe his circle. Yet another spoke of an 'oligarchy' running the town, and evidently regarded himself as part of it. One respondent drew up a list of the inner ring of 'influentials' name by name, most of whom were included in the sample, and who, he assured me, enjoyed close relations with one another. Implicit in much of the evidence provided by the interviews was the consciousness that the sample occupied leading positions and shared many close associations. Their superior status is quite as subjective as it is objective. Not that such connections are wholly exclusive or exhaustive – they are not aloof, *grands seigneurs*, despite the testimony that 'one' just didn't meet local authority people at the kind of parties 'one' attended, or that such people and the Town Clerk 'might inhabit different worlds'. The sense of difference and yet of non-aloofness is conveyed by a comment that 'there is a great social

[1] The persistent deference among Welsh working-class people towards middle-class people is strikingly illustrated in Brennan, *et al.*, *Social Change in South-West Wales*, pp. 105–6. See also the trends in Newcastle under Lyme; Bealey, *et al.*, *Constituency Politics*, p. 388. And, generally, W. G. Runciman in the *Listener*, 22 July 1965, pp. 115–18.

range in [the village where the speaker lives] and I enjoy meeting them and doing things with them' – like presiding over the Legion branch and the management of the village hall.

The sources of this influence and superiority in the social hierarchy are manifold and complex. Amongst them is the fact that they possess social prestige and important friendships and many are endowed with a kind of traditional legitimacy based on family descent – it is not uncommon for some firms to employ the grandchildren of people who formerly worked for the grandfather of the present directorate.[1] Many are experts in some field of professional or business skill and besides are experienced in bearing responsibility in administration and in making judgements in weighty affairs. They also often feel themselves and are acknowledged to fill representative roles as spokesmen of important associations, firms, societies, industries, interest groups or trades, which gives them weight, authority and receptive audiences as well as psychic reassurance and stamina. Moreover, many are closely associated with the leadership of institutions of real economic power, and if it is true that government is today ubiquitous, it is also true, as S. H. Beer, for example, has pointed out, that manifold interests are involved in, and influential upon, government.

It could be that though differentiated in these ways from most of the community, the economic and social notables resemble the political notables, the party representatives on the Council, if we compare the two groups in their occupational and social prestige, wealth, links with the leading families, class affiliations and social

[1] But it is doubtful whether in Bristol one could clearly assign individuals to either a 'traditional' status system to a 'nontraditional' systemp cf. Stacey, *Tradition and Change*, pp. 21–37.

status. However, it turns out that the membership of the political class and the membership of the economic and social élite are pretty distinct. This phenomenon is recognised by the notables themselves; one says, 'There are few, if any, top business people on the Council in Bristol', and another, 'There is not a complete cross-section on the Council – the top business social stratum is missing.' Indeed, only about three members of the Council could be said, in terms of these characteristics, to resemble an 'average' member of the sample, while of the latter probably only some 10 per cent could be said more or less wholly to resemble, in their social qualities, some of the Council. The latter comprises predominantly people in manual, white collar, small shopkeeping or lower managerial jobs, plus a few professional men and better-known businessmen. The point is illustrated by Table 38, which analyses into socio-economic groups the 84 members of Bristol's Council elected in recent years. Unfortunately lack of positive information precludes distinguishing between categories 1 and 2 and between 3 and 4. In vulgar class-terms, the Council is mainly composed of working- and lower-middle-class and some middle-class people, whereas the sample is overwhelmingly middle and upper class. Further, without the weight of their political office, not more than three councillors, who enjoy business and professional positions and family connections similar in reputation to those so common in the sample, compare in their social eminence with even the middle ranks of the sample. Few other councillors would have the same standing as the less substantial members of the sample. Outside the political sector, most councillors almost wholly lack the positions of authority in commerce, business or the professions which invest so many members of the sample with an aura of respect, lending them so much authority and attracting deference from others.[1]

TABLE 38[2]   Councillors elected in 1962, 1963 and 1964;
by socio-economic groups

| Group | No. | % |
|---|---|---|
| 1. Large and small employers and managers (1 and 2) | 26 | 31 |
| 2. Professional workers; employed and self-employed (3 and 4) | 12 | 14 |
| 3. Intermediate independent non-manual (5) | 9 | 11 |
| 4. Junior non-manual (6) | 11 | 13 |
| 5. Skilled manual (9) | 20 | 24 |
| 6. Semi-skilled manual (10) | 3 | 4 |
| 7. Own account non-professional (12) | 1 | 1 |
| 8. Unclassified | 2 | 2 |
| 9. Total | 84 | 100 |

An important implication of these facts is that the sample is not, therefore, merely a sample of eminent people who are active in voluntary but not council affairs; it is also a somewhat skewed sample of the local economic and social notables as such, whether active or inactive, since there is a boycott of council membership by almost all the economic and social notables. If we can find a hypothesis accounting for the avoidance of council service by active notables, it may apply *a fortiori* to the economic and social élites in general.

To establish that members of the sample are not councillors and that the group occupies a generally superior position in society is merely to have drawn the

[1] They are merely 'public persons' as J. M. Lee would put it (*Social Leaders*, p. 5). It seems highly unlikely that Bristolians would name so high a proportion of councillors among the city's 'influentials' as was said to be among Glossop's 'influentials'; Birch, *Small-Town Politics*, p. 42.
[2] See Table 1.

rough beginnings of the lineaments of a map of its relations with the political system. What is the extent and nature of political participation by members of the sample? When questioned about voting in recent local and national elections all but four indicated that they voted at the local level (and residents of rural districts are sometimes faced with uncontested elections), and all but one in the national poll of 1964. It is notorious that respondents are often excessively optimistic not only about their intention to vote, but even about the simple historical facts of their voting records.[1] However, assuming that notables are no more deceitful or forgetful than the general public, a phenomenally high rate of turn-out is apparently characteristic of the sample.

Table 39, which follows, gives details about other kinds of political activity. Over three-quarters belong to a party, supporting it with money, however little else may be contributed. In fact over a quarter do more than pay a subscription; it may be little or it may be much – but they do some canvassing, drive a car, man a committee room, speak on behalf of a candidate at election time or occasionally attend a party meeting. In addition another 14 per cent hold, or have recently held, office at ward, constituency or city level in the party of their choice. And about a tenth of the sample have filled elective office on some sort of local Council. Those who have been active and office-holders together amount to 41 per cent. Over 60, or nearly 80 per cent, are, or have recently been, active in one or other of all these ways.

[1] See, for example, Maud Report, III 78; and Bealey and Bartholomew in *British Journal of Sociology*, XIII 284; and Birch, *Small-Town Politics*, p. 98. On the other hand, L. J. Sharpe found a close correspondence between the proportion of his sample claiming to vote and the proportion of the sample actually voting; L. J. Sharpe, *A Metropolis Votes* (London School of Economics, 1962) p. 58.

Even among the fifth who appear to be quite inactive, one or two number M.P.s as their friends or have politically active wives.

TABLE 39　Types of political activity

|  | No. | % |
| --- | --- | --- |
| 1. Present, recent party members – pay subscription | 59 | 76 |
| 2. Members of Constitutional Club[1] | 28 | 36 |
| 3. Active party members – canvass, drive, speak, meet | 21 | 27 |
| 4. Office in ward, constituency or borough | 11 | 14 |
| 5. Served on rural district council, county council, or borough council | 7 | 9 |
| 6. Served on parish council | 2 | 3 |

Although many sought to deprecate the 'small' extent of their party political activity, this can only be in comparison either with the standard of their own business or voluntary commitments, or with what might be expected of a would-be or actual political representative. In comparison with any sample of the general public the evidence shows a very high rate of participation and interest in party politics.[2] The avoidance of council service is clearly not due to a total alienation from the society or the political system as a whole,

[1] A Conservative club, usually electorally apathetic as a body, but it provided canvassers for the Conservatives in Bristol North-East in 1955. Milne and Mackenzie, *Marginal Seat*, p. 19.

[2] Almond and Verba, *Civic Culture*, p. 161 n.; Rose, *Politics in England*, p. 94; J. Blondel, *Voters, Parties and Leaders* (Penguin, 1963) chs 3, 4 and 5; Birch, *Small-Town Politics*, pp. 95–8; Bealey, *et al.*, *Constituency Politics*, pp. 95–8. L. J. Sharpe found no greater propensity to vote amongst the educated and the middle class than amongst others in London local elections; *A Metropolis Votes*, pp. 74–5. Similar findings are reported from a Scottish constituency; Budge and Urwin, *Scottish Political Behaviour*, p. 80.

which, they evidently feel, is reasonably sensitive and responsive to their needs and norms. This is especially true of the Conservative Party which secures the adherence of the great majority. Table 4 showed that 85 per cent of those giving usable information support the Conservatives, and to many of them the machinery and officials of the party, whether local branches of the national organisation, or the local body known as the 'Citizen' party, which carries the Conservative banner on Bristol's Council, are readily accessible, formally and informally. Their loyalty is by no means unwavering; one or two have spoiled their ballots or voted for the Liberal in protest against their sitting Conservative Member of Parliament. One treasurer of his local Conservative Party denies that he is 'active' – he 'hates' it. A subscriber to the Conservative Party occasionally helps the Liberal candidate, and has no strong party convictions; he feels 'there is a lot of good in a lot of people'.[1] They entertain quite a wide range of opinion, and most have strong reservations about political life and politicians, but in no other party could they feel as comfortably at home.

However, the party and electoral machinery provide the main and most cherished avenues for contact with the local authority for only a minority. The manner in which the manifold powers of the authority are used can closely concern them. City policy and standards of efficiency have an impact upon all, and may be considerable upon some. Planning decisions affect business premises; traffic causes personal problems and influences business efficiency; city development touches the aesthetic sensibilities; a close interest in voluntary

---

[1] Milne and Mackenzie tell of a Bristol office-holder in the Young Conservatives who was not a paid-up member of the party (*Marginal Seat*, p. 14); and see above, p. 32.

work of, say, a welfare or an educational character, can often be intimately affected by municipal policy; professional interests may be engaged, as with the doctor dealing at top level with the Public Health Department over the establishment of a health centre in the city. Where all these things are concerned members of the sample often make swift and extensive use of their easy access to the municipal authority. Not all enjoy such accessibility, a few have encountered barriers and suspicion; nor can every approach expect to be crowned with unqualified success. Not all are very clear as to how to make these approaches but most are, in quite some detail and subtlety. Tables 19 and 24 have shown something of these contacts.

The 6 per cent in Table 19 who say they do not follow council affairs greatly understates the number who do not continuously try to keep up to date. Yet the table suggests that there is no group in the city outside the Council except perhaps a few highly engaged party militants who are likely to have more extensive, frequent and meaningful contacts with the authority. In the bottom six lines over half are shown to derive information, whether general or specific to their interests, from councillors. But according to the Maud Survey only 17 per cent of all informants had 'ever' contacted a councillor in their districts, and only 29 per cent even of socio-economic group 1.[1] The variety of *milieux* in which these contacts are made is suggestive of the way the circles in which councillors and council officials move, and the circles in which the sample moves, though not the same, intersect at numerous different levels and points.

Table 20 illustrates the degree of contact between the sample and the representative machinery as it functions

[1] Maud Report, III 52–3.

formally through the Council and its committees. Almost nine out of ten have never attended a council meeting, but even fewer of the general public have done so.[1] On the other hand about half of the sample have had some direct dealings with one or more committees, sometimes as committee members if ex-councillors, or as part of the important joint Downs committee, whose fourteen members are divided equally between councillors and members of the Merchant Venturers Society, and are together responsible for the administration of approximately 400 acres of park-land near the heart of Bristol comprising the Downs; twelve of the sample have served on this committee. Close contact with committees, too, is experienced by notables as citizens deeply interested in educational issues, as businessmen in relation, say, to planning matters, or as voluntary workers interested in, say, youth affairs on a professional level. Without exaggerating the strength of these (very often) temporary and usually *ad hoc* connections, it is apparent that no random sample of the public has such extensive and intimate commerce of this type with the Council.[2] In addition they meet councillors and officials as fellow-members in clubs, on the magistrates' bench, on hospital management committees and so forth. Twenty-three members of the sample and 7 councillors are Bristol J.P.s; 28 of the sample and 14 councillors belong to the Constitutional Club; 23 members of the sample and 10 councillors belong to the university court. Social contact of this type with the chief officers is perhaps less frequent, but according to a Rotary officer, some half-dozen chief officials of the authority

[1] Maud Report, iii 57, table 83.
[2] According to the Social Survey only 6 per cent of the public had been in touch with a councillor in the whole of the previous year; Maud Report, iii 54, table 78.

belong to that society, as do 14 people in the sample.

Just how extensive is this acquaintanceship? Table 21 attempted a rough measure and it shows half our informants claiming to know ten or more councillors and four, five, or more top officials, Only three said they 'really' didn't know either any councillors or officials, all three in fact have had some recent contact with one or the other; all three display peculiarly deep horror of the political system. There are clearly degrees of 'knowing', but the great majority of these relationships seem to fall between the barest nodding acquaintanceship and the close personal friendship between, say, men who shoot together on Saturdays. Of these latter there are very few indeed. Some councillors and officials are known to medical members of the sample as patients; to clerical members as part of their spiritual flock; acquaintanceships may be struck up on the London train or among the Bristol Savages. Most councillors known to notables are Citizens, but many stress also their acquaintance with a handful of older Labour leaders, who have been chairmen of committees, Lord Mayors, fellow participants in social municipal functions – welcoming a Royal personage to the city, for example – or colleagues on the bench or on hospital management committees. Relations with an occasional Citizen member may blossom in less formal circumstances, at the Constitutional Club or the Bristol Club,[1] or sometimes in business situations. Whatever the quality and the salience to them of these contacts, almost all the sample has far closer and more extensive relations with many of the men in the municipal authority than almost any other conceivable group of the general populace.

Table 22 showed that about 40 per cent of the sample

[1] To which fourteen of the sample and three or four councillors belong.

rarely or never get in touch with an official or councillor by visiting, telephoning or writing, but about the same proportion have monthly, fortnightly or weekly contact with councillors or officers, either personally or through a close subordinate. Compared with other members of society, this is a phenomenally frequent rate of inter-action. Indeed one man himself said that due to his ability to contact people he regards himself 'as a Sidney Stanley'. Of the national sample only 26 per cent had made contact, on the average twice, with the local authority in the previous year, and the occasions seem to have been to make either complaints, or inquiries, or other highly personal transactions.[1]

Those of the notables who have most frequent contacts with Bristol Corporation are concerned mainly with business matters affected by planning, the engineer's department, city estate administration, housing policy, the operation of the docks and so on. Contacts by some people over social welfare problems are frequent but, in most non-business spheres like education, rather intermittent; an example of an exception being a doctor in weekly touch with the public health and children's committees and departments.

Nearly a third of the notables leave the contact-making to others, usually subordinates in their firms. About a half of them stress the regularity and frequency of their contacts, implying that no special approach is necessitated by new problems, for these are dealt with as they arise through normal (for them) dealings with officials, departments, committees and chairmen. Matter-of-course and friendly relations – eased and symbolised by such customs as a firm's engineer entertaining the City Engineer to lunch every year or so – with the adminis-trative machine are actively sought after and indeed are

[1] Maud Report, III 49, tables 67 and 70.

E

necessary to a large part of the sample in reference either to their business or to cherished goals in other spheres of interest. A few stress particular tactics which it is sometimes prudent to follow, like picking the 'right' person (official or committee member) with whom to make the initial contact; or deciding the appropriate stage at which to commit oneself to writing; in such circumstances extensive knowledge of the personnel and operating characteristics of the Council becomes invaluable in avoiding offence and difficulty. Consciousness of the value of such tactics is significant of their familiarity. Small numbers make contacts through some such organisation as the Bristol Council of Social Service, or Rotary, or a trade association. Less formal contacts are made through councillor colleagues on voluntary or public bodies. Thus attention to a traffic bollard may be obtained by a word with an alderman who is a fellow-member of a hospital management committee. In other words, an 'old-boy network' is employed; opportunities are used to insinuate ideas in realms quite other than that with which the immediate occasion is concerned. Altogether, some 90 per cent of the sample are reasonably satisfied with the quality of their links with the authority, whether they are frequent, rare, trivial or intimate. Indeed, two-thirds asserted this positively to be the case, while only a tenth either found their council connections unsatisfactory or want none. Against that, 13 per cent went out of their way to emphasise the helpfulness of the Corporation. All in all, the evidence suggests that no other social group can rival this one in its experience of council techniques and people, nor in the availability to it of various channels of communication with the Corporation and its members. Very few in the sample lack some contact with councillors, officials or committees, while for a sizeable minority such interaction is frequent and the relationships fairly intimate. Familiarity with, and knowledge of, council operations, policies and modes of working, as well as the personnel, is extensive.

Accessibility indeed is more or less assured for these people purely as economic and social notables; according to one witness, 'the Corporation will always discuss things if you have integrity and standing'. On the other hand, a self-made businessman, of Labour sympathies, remarked on the difficulty he had in making initial contacts with chief officers. Now that he is not only relatively successful in business but also associates with some bigger established figures in the sample through a common interest in helping handicapped people, he finds access to the Corporation has become much easier.

But a note of caution should be sounded here; many business and professional people like to retain a certain element of distance in their relations with the authority. There is a tradition of probity that makes many agree with the man who said, 'Sometimes it could be embarrassing if one got one's feet in too far – if one knew people and affairs too well. I always try to get things through on their merits, by the direct approach. I'm no politician.' Moreover both the formal bureaucratic structure and the formal political structure are extremely tough and can be very resistant. They do not simply dissolve into a miasma of informal relationships with outside individuals and groups – far from it.[1]

---

[1] Thus, in comparison with Seattle's formal government, D. C. Miller found Bristol's Corporation more directly concerned in solving civic problems, and the voluntary organisations more fluid than in Seattle; *American Journal of Sociology*, LXIV 307. The large degree of autonomy enjoyed by sub-systems that

And yet access to committees, departments or chairmen is of a very different order of participation in the decision-making process from the only resource available and widely used by most citizens – voting; also from the purely personal complaints and inquiries resorted to by a small minority; and even from the influence of a few active party-workers. The sympathy or criticism with which these outside views will be received depends on many factors – for instance on how well they fit into an often rather ill-defined policy or ideology. It is, however, significant that the Social Survey pointed up the importance to councillors of 'informal contacts' in getting to know about public needs or aspirations, especially as many councillors see the smallest handful of electors every few weeks.[1] Consequently the importance of the frequency, persistence and intimacy of the notables' contacts is much enhanced.

Normally, except when the object is merely to seek information, a contact in this context is an attempt to influence the decision-making process, even if only to speed it up or to slow it down. Often, indeed, there is hope of influencing the actual content of the decision, whether it be in the realm of planning, the placing of housing contracts, developments in welfare, or in education policy and so on. It is usually simply a matter of 'give and take', of mutual accommodation, reached during normal business relations; 'the Corporation wants so much from our firm that they're always

R. Rose detects is apparent in the political and economic systems in Bristol, and their mutual relations at top levels often consist of co-operative bargaining; but in other areas of social life in which power and status are distributed the autonomy and equality are less evident; Rose, *Politics in England*, pp. 120–5.

[1] Maud Report, II 223–7.

anxious to help us, and an ordinary conversation is best'. Such accommodations might, for example, take the form of agreement by the Planning Department to provide an alternative site as a *quid pro quo* if a firm cheerfully accepts the Department's prohibition upon development on an existing site, and other bargains are struck by large building firms with respect to housing-contracts or renovation or maintenance of council property. 'Our company deals with the Law committee which on the whole is pretty good; it has to be cultivated so that it understands our problems, but it is very ready to do so; the chairman is very worthy and sensible, and his deputy was in [another company with which the informant is connected].' According to another partici-pant, 'one goes to see the chairman of the planning com-mittee, his anxieties have to be allayed, and one can do this face to face. There are no difficulties in dealing with the Council, you have to treat them in the right way, to tell them what you want before you do it'; this was apropos of an institution of higher education about which some on the Council entertained unhappy feelings that this was precisely what it did not do.

Inevitably, because these are very largely the people with whom the local authority must directly deal, as owners and managers of property, business or profes-sional practices within the city, they influence decisions. These cannot be made by councillors in a vacuum, however thoroughly legitimised may be the power of the representatives by the suffrages of the people,[1] and however well advised they are by informed officials. There are the leaders of voluntary bodies, too; they approach the Council less like equal powers and more as

[1] Who on the whole accept the legitimacy of these relations between interests and government; Rose, *Politics in England*, p. 44.

suppliants, but then they are also more independent of the Council than often businessmen can afford to be. For, though their *locus standi* is less firm, their personal fortunes are less dependent upon favourable responses from the Council; for example, if they are speaking for some such body as the N.S.P.C.C. Strength of personality, contacts with ministry officials, links with national headquarters of the organisation may count for a good deal in this situation.

How often such involvement in decision-making becomes 'pressure', in the sense that a kind of sanction is employed against the authority to cause it to come to a decision that is, in some fashion and degree, to its disadvantage and at which it would not otherwise have arrived, is very difficult to establish; so too is the frequency of success. The evidence is scrappy and unsystematic. That resort is had to other means of contact or influence than the normal day-to-day channels is clear even from the replies analysed in Table 24. Something like a tenth stipulate that they exert no pressure, and no doubt the proportion who use no extraordinary means of influence beyond their routine contacts, or, indeed, no contacts at all, is even larger. But 5 per cent did, without even being directly asked, say they exert pressure, and the various techniques and channels detailed in the table gives the impression that rather more are so engaged on occasion.

One respondent told the story of a case in which, he said, 'the officials went back on what they had told' him. He threatened to appeal against the subsequent planning decision and the Corporation retreated. Another claimed that 'one or two contacts in the Citizen Party will put our point of view to their party' – but in fact, in a planning matter of particular importance to them, the firm in question had its hopes wholly disappointed, the Citizens on the committee refusing to vote. Access through a body such as a trade association, Rotary, the Chamber of Commerce or the Council of Social Service may be purely a matter of convenience, but sometimes it may add political force to an argument.

A quarter of the sample count the local Press as sympathetic to them, and letters, reports or inspired editorials printed in the newspaper can put pressure on the authority. They may be published as 'kites' to gauge public reaction, if any. Of the two local papers, the *Evening Post* is the major one, and though in the past it has opposed the speedy extension of compre-hensive secondary education it would be difficult to sustain an argument that it is in the pocket of Conser-vative or any other interest, since it adopts more liberal or 'progressive' lines on many other issues and the owner-ship is local.[1] Four of those interviewed are directors of the company; all denied any influence upon editorial policy, but it was made clear that the paper pays more heed to an issue raised with it by somebody who is 'influential', and will do more to keep the pot boiling with editorials, articles and so on in such a case.

Yet amongst those with Press contacts, a rather ambivalent attitude was not uncommon. Some are quite confident of their ability to handle the Press, though one very shortly after his interview badly got his fingers burnt. One man enthused over the successful help the Press had given in enlisting the aid of the local authority in a cultural venture behind which he has been the driving force. Another related an episode during which he had inspired a report which had stimulated the granting of permission to erect a sports building. Several talked of 'cultivating' their relationship with the Press,

[1] In recent years it has become slowly but steadily more Con-servative in sympathy.

to make more favourable the 'image' the papers build up of their enterprises. Some groups, such as the doctors, have a designated Press liaison officer. On the other hand – and this is where the ambiguity comes in – there is little evidence that they can sway the Press by unsubtle means. According to the testimony of one man whose business puts a lot of advertising into the *Evening Post*, they have no impact on editorial policy. The tones of respect, even fear, or downright dislike of the Press colouring other comments rather support this view. The fact that the newspapers are almost wholly swayed by their criterion of 'newsworthiness' is cause for resentment. 'We often go to the Press for publicity for a good cause, but they are not interested because it is not "news"', complained one man. Others acknowledged help from the Press in matters concerning youth or the arts, but they still felt it to be 'suspect'. Some rather scorned it, alleging its unreliability in reporting. Numbers have very little active relationship with the Press at all, and those who feel they can handle it and count upon it confidently as an ally are decidedly in a minority.

There is also recourse, in the search for friends, to the use of *ad hoc* or specially oriented pressure-groups. Policy, national and local, regarding the future development of local broadcasting was closely watched by a group three of whose members are in the sample. Then there are the groups of retail traders based upon particular shopping areas – the Broadmead Traders, the Queen's Road Traders' Association – who continuously watch over their members' interests *vis-à-vis* the Corporation, with special reference to rating, parking-meters and traffic regulations, and jump into more active life in the Press and with special meetings and statements when they feel the Council is propounding a 'threat' to, or is neglecting, their interests. The Chamber of Commerce has recently been trying to improve its relations generally with the Council, especially regarding the pattern of docks administration in which they feel the trading and using community should have more say.[1]

However, the typical relationship between notables and the local political system is not usually one of pressure, but commonly one of businesslike co-operation, bargaining, 'give and take', in enterprises in which both or all sides are recognised to have legitimate, if sometimes somewhat differing, interests. The element of influence, or power, in the relationship is generally muted. This limitation is assisted by a view of society, shared by many, which sees the various bodies, like the Trades Council, a voluntary welfare organisation, the Chamber of Commerce, a firm, the local authority, as operating 'in different spheres'. One businessman, talking about the problems of relations with the Council as seen from the point of view of the Chamber of Commerce, said 'the two political parties form a sort of club and are both against involving industry with them'. Another, very management-conscious businessman, said, 'I should think seriously about politics only if it threatened the business.' On the other hand a high trade union official pointed out that 'there is a sort of code on each side [of industry] not to use pressure tactics – for example we don't approach the Labour members on the

[1] The *Evening Post* reported on 14 July 1966 that the Chamber was currently concerned with Bristol Airport (dissatisfaction with road-access), Canons Marsh development (new harbour bridge should swing to admit craft to the Frome), Old Market (liaison with traders over redevelopment), the municipally-owned great house and park at Ashton Court (concern over its future), education (career liaison), and motorways (pressure on Whitehall to speed programme).

E 2

docks committee, so as not to embarrass them'. Another businessman rather aptly summed up succinctly the point of view of a great many when he said, 'One is reasonable in one's claims.' Thus though the accessibility for notables to the local political system is much more intimate, easier and more various than it is for the general public, exploitation is rarely pushed to its maximum, and a decorous and useful balance in the system is maintained.[1]

Their role, then, within the local system, far from being characteristically an abstentionist one, is an active participating one. Or, one might say, their interest in the 'output' of the system is large and their 'input' is correspondingly high. Their relationships with both the appointed and the elected sides of the local authority are so often extensive and close that they are of a different kind from those enjoyed by most of the electorate. Typically, to a high degree, these are 'insiders'; not necessarily in the sense that they manipulate the machinery and personnel, but in the sense that they are an integral part of the means by which the political system is related to the economic and social systems.

[1] This relationship appears to be something like that suggested by J. Blondel as subsisting between the larger firms and central government (*Voters, Parties and Leaders*, pp. 166, 222).

# CHAPTER 7

# Some Explanations for the Notables' Non-Participation as Councillors

SOME analysis and discussion of the views expressed by the sample themselves as to the causes of their non-participation as representatives on the local Council appeared in Chapter 3. The main single expressed objection – their lack of available time – is not a satisfactory explanation, bearing in mind the large amount of time and attention they choose to devote to other activities which appear to be comparable in many respects. To say this is not by any means to reject out of hand their own explanation. With its remorseless, highly organised machinery, and the multiplicity and importance of its tasks, local government in a large city is very demanding, and its demands are not easily evaded or conveniently fitted into other needs.[1] Cuts in the size and numbers of the council committees, and greater delegation of authority to officers would clearly appeal to many in the sample, not only as managerial reforms desirable in themselves, but also as time-saving techniques in the peculiar context of English local

[1] Though it has been pointed out that socio-economic group 1 councillors in fact do this to a greater extent than others; Maud Report, II 296.

government. Some such modification could well have a marginal effect in persuading one or two members of the sample to stand. Testimony of ex-councillors in the sample lends support to this view. But other responses suggest that the effect would be quite marginal.

Again, the testimony from my informants gives little encouragement to the idea that the other main type of reform which is fashionable – the reconstruction of local government into much larger authorities – would have a very marked effect in recruiting this type of person. There is evidence from the interviews that regionalism of this kind is favourably regarded by some members of the sample as an administrative improvement; that to a few such a change could make local government more appealing – and one or two were quite positive that they would consider the notion very seriously indeed if such changes were made. Even if a mere handful were to join such a regional council the proportion of this type of person serving could well be considerably increased, since a regional structure would severely reduce the total number of council places to be filled. But since their total numbers are small and their present council participation is practically nil it is not clear that the absolute rise in the numbers of their representatives gained by this expedient – whatever else might be gained – would be very great. The highly middle-class character of the House of Commons is a suggestive parallel; but the relative absence, even from there, of people who have made big names in business, industry or commerce is significant. In any case, our problem – the sociological problem of the continued abstention of the great majority of the sample and notables like them – would still remain.

What we seek is a theory of non-participation, or rather a theory to account for a pattern of behaviour which includes considerable but limited participation. Participation in the political system is prompted both by group norms and interests, and by individual interests or psychic needs. The previous chapter established that we are dealing with people who, in many respects, comprise a group, or rather a sample of a group, and individual explanations would be inadequate – the explanation of why the political behaviour of this type of person does not include council membership cannot be in individual terms. Other research suggests that people of much education, high status, considerable wealth, do participate more – in voting, party membership, electoral activity, in representation – than other people. We have seen that many are involved as insiders in their relations not simply with local politicians but also in the day-to-day administration. Why is the line drawn at council membership? Motivating them in their extensive activity is often a sense of duty and a sense of their traditional as well as of their modern roles; but it may be generally assumed that in explanations of political conduct there will also be a group interest at stake. There seems to be no reason why we should not assume that members of the sample have a keen sense of their own interests. The almost unanimous preference for the Conservative Party and the considerable activity in its support lends credence to this view. If so, the further assumption seems to follow that members of the group will wish to influence the implementation, if not the making, of policy by whatever means they are aware of lying to hand and which they are not inhibited from employing. These means, looked at in Chapter 6, and these inhibitions are important among the factors which decide the contours of the pattern of their behaviour.

Several theorists of community power-structure

suggest that high-status managers and owners of large professional, commercial and industrial concerns do not take leading representative positions in the formal political system of the local community simply because they do not require to do so to get their way. Why should this be so? Firstly, it may be because the local political structure is so limited in the scope of its activities as to be more or less irrelevant to large-scale professional or business enterprises, assuming that these form the core of the interests of the group.

Then there are three further hypotheses behind which is the assumption that if the local political system, contrary to the first hypothesis, disposes of real power which can on occasion damage the widely defined interests of the local economic and social leadership and their concerns, these people, of whom the sample comprises some, would quickly find their way on to the Council in order to control or check it, except in certain circumstances. Firstly, it may be that the local political system has powers and so forth, but these can be directed or thwarted by the central political power, with which large enterprise and people of high social status have such *rapport* that they can ensure that local politicians are not allowed to harm their interests. Or, secondly, it may be that the local political system disposes of powers and allocates values, but the relations of the economic and social notables with local political notables – leading political representatives – is such that the latter do not act so as to damage the former's interests. Finally, a third hypothesis might be that the local political system can and does touch their interests but the level and type of their actual participation – their utilisation of their access to the party machinery and to the administration described in the previous chapter – is so effective that their interests are not injured in ways unacceptable to their views and their expectations of the political system.

That in certain circumstances it is no mere *a priori* fantasy to suspect that there might be an urge positively to act upon and within the representative system, in order to protect interests if damage to them threatened to reach intolerable levels is suggested by certain comments of the sample. Several said they might later seek membership of a Council if there was a call, or some sort of crisis. One or two made the point that they tend to use their vote negatively, against 'undesirables'. One active Conservative named a very big company which, he says, 'places' members of the firm on the Council, to keep the latter 'sweet'; there are, however, a lot of improbabilities about this. Again, a businessman says he has seriously contemplated standing for the Council because of his distress at its inadequate concern for, and information about, the place of the arts and culture in the community's life.

Taking up the very first hypothesis, one of the possibilities placed before the sample as an explanation for their absence from the Council was that the local authority was deficient in power, which could mean that its status as an activity would be low, that its potential achievements would not be worth expending time and energy upon to secure and that it could do little to make or mar their interests. Considering the prevalence of this criticism amongst the *cognoscenti*, and the fears that such power as remains is being eroded from various directions, it is somewhat surprising that a mere handful of the sample did take the view that local government had become largely a 'rubber-stamp' for Whitehall (Tables 26, 27, 28, 29). According to one man, 'Power has tended to disappear from the local level; so much of the money comes from Whitehall that it is largely controlled by Whitehall, so it is less interesting to businessmen.' According to another, 'On any major issue, like the Portbury Dock scheme, we have to get London's agreement; if the city Council had much stronger powers it could have twisted somebody's arm with effect.' Some believe (Table 26) that apathy at the polls can be attributed to a popular belief that there is not much effective power at local level, without, however, themselves subscribing to this view. In fact only 12 per cent, when asked to evaluate the Council's work, suggested that it is too circumscribed by financial and central limitations (Table 28), while several went out of their way to emphasise the adequacy of local powers. To some extent this is due to their relatively conservative anti-government system of thought. The Maud Report shows that quite a lot of councillors want more powers and greater use of existing powers. The attitudes of the notables suggest less consciousness of the need for intervention, and that they are more insulated than councillors from pressures to act. It is significant that the Maud Committee found that employers and professional councillors were less likely than other socio-economic groups to seek an extension of council powers.[1] However, this is only part of the explanation for the general satisfaction with the scope of local government; it seems to be generally based upon a feeling amongst these men of influence that the local government of this large city can in fact do important things. For example, one of those frequently suggested by other members of the sample as an admirable potential member of the Council if he could be recruited, himself said, 'I've not shirked the local authority because it is not worth while, but because I have not the time.' And, of course, few of the organisations upon which they lavish so much time do

[1] Maud Report, II 160–1.

possess such large powers for good or ill as a local authority has at its disposal.

Moreover, when asked what kind of problems enlightened men should be anticipating as facing Bristol within the next ten or fifteen years, a wide variety of answers was given. Here it is not so much the specific content of these answers that is of interest as the fact that, firstly, they do cover a wide range of problems, moral, economic, welfare and environmental planning (Table 29); secondly, many such problems are of undoubted importance on any scale of values; and, thirdly, about three-quarters of the sample feel that the city's municipal government is of direct relevance to the solution of the problems, even if doubts might be expressed either about its capacity for the task, or about anybody at all finding a solution. Local government in a city of this magnitude is not felt by many even of this sample to be negligible. Indeed, even some of the criticisms suggest the opposite: one of the more conservative would like to cut it down to dealing with the drains and refuse-disposal. Demands that it be reformed to rise to business standards of efficiency assume the importance of its functions. One or two asserted that the contribution of top social and economic notables even to Bristol was greater in their present roles as leaders of large companies immersed in various national affairs than their contribution as councillors could be. But many implied that named individual notables, often in the sample, would find in serving the municipality tasks commensurate only with their high abilities, if it were not, unfortunately, that they lack the time. Criticism of the competence of serving councillors underlines the same point. All in all, whether they are right or wrong in their judgement, there is very little evidence here that many notables are deterred from standing for the

Council by the thought that its work does not encompass sufficiently important affairs.[1] This is one reason for thinking that expectations that an increment of power to a regional system of local government will stimulate the recruitment of local notables may be disappointed.

Thus the Council has power; it can do important things; it can do things which affect many of the sample in significant ways, and they feel this. For part of our explanation then, we must look in the direction of the other hypotheses, to see how the notables cope with this situation without joining the Council. A goodly minority have close and continuous relations with the Council on a business or professional footing and are intimately engaged in the execution of its policy, and many others are closely concerned with the administration and the results of policy-making.[2] In these and in other ways, though some may encounter barriers and most of these transactions, though agreeably concluded, are the product of bargaining and compromise, most feel they enjoy reasonably easy and adequate access to officials, departments and committees. It is true that one informant testified that in some areas of welfare work with which he is concerned, had he been a member of the Council, results might well have been expedited. This view is uncommon and something of a mystique of the voluntariness of non-Council voluntary work helps to keep the two apart; a diligent woman denied that her goals might be more easily achieved via council membership: 'Objectivity is important in my way of think-

[1] Investigators who found that non-voters in Newcastle under Lyme did not ascribe their non-voting to a belief in the unimportance of local government preferred to reject their finding; Bealey, *et al.*, *Constituency Politics*, p. 246.

[2] Chapter 6. Of course, extensive interests of this kind will be affected by only a small minority of items on the typical agenda of a monthly council meeting.

ing; I have probably been of more use to the ——
committee as a member of a voluntary body than as one
among many councillors.' On the whole, they feel their
wants are accommodated without the extremity of
election to the Council, or, at least, the allocation of
values by the political system accords reasonably well
with their expectations. This is no doubt part of the
explanation why people of this sort do not find it
necessary to seek positions of formal power on the
Council – our last hypothesis is at least partially true
(see pages 142–3 above).

But it might be that these expectations are not pitched
very high. How far are these matters at the core of the
needs and values of the majority of these notables? If they
are continuous and quite central concerns then a firmer
and closer relationship with the decision-making of
the political system might well seem desirable. It seems
unlikely, however, that problems such as planning,
traffic, voluntary social work, reform in local administrative arrangements and so forth are the main concerns
of more than a small fraction for any long periods of
time. What is clearly their most fundamental pre-
occupation is the prosperity and fame of their industrial,
commercial or professional enterprises. This is no
*a priori* judgement, but one based upon their most
emphatic statements as to the primacy of their business
and career interests (Table 11). Basically, for them the
most important items in public policy are economic
events. In so far as municipal activities impinge on
industrial or on commercial development, comment is
largely favourable; on the possibility of coming to agreement with the planners, on the efficiency with which the
financial affairs of the city are managed by the
Treasurer, and even on the traffic problem it is generally
recognised that the administration is doing its best, not

without success. But economic trends form a sphere where local government powers and functions rarely have crucial relevance – it is central government or the market which are held responsible. Here the problem is that Bristol's political system is, in many respects, a very open one, subject to national influences and set very firmly in a national context. The difficulties thus posed are redoubled by the extension of the economic – and political – interests of the sample very far beyond Bristol's municipal boundaries.

To assess the sample's relations with central government requires further research, but it is clear that some, at least, are not unfamiliar with Whitehall's corridors, either because of present activities or through contacts cherished from an earlier period of service in the war or post-war years. One or two are ready to get immediately in touch with senior Ministry officials to exert pressure on lower levels in the hierarchy in the region; one or two mentioned their acquaintance with cabinet ministers. One chairman of a medium-sized manufacturing-business is positive that two or three of the dominant firms use their influence with the Board of Trade to discourage new industrial development in Bristol in order to check rises in local wage-levels. But while these are hints of interstitial efforts to influence local development by means of pressure exerted upon central government there is little evidence that such a course is habitual and established or successful in large affairs.

Indeed, regarding local economic matters, the economic and social notables seem to be normally at one with the local political notables in dealing with the national political system. The municipal Council, of whatever party complexion,[1] is strongly influenced to

[1] In part exception to this normal solidarity, the Labour group on the Council is having difficulty in choosing between the Labour

sympathise with local business even if 'only' because of its concern with employment and general prosperity. Bristol Council will not strongly campaign against cigarette-smoking, out of respect for important tobacco-interests, both union and employer; and concern over the Concorde and TSR2 crises has been as much with the implications for local prestige and employment as with presumed national economic needs. The esteem in which the leadership of the municipal Port of Bristol Authority is held by Bristol businessmen has on the whole been enhanced by the campaign, which they have supported, launched by the P.B.A. to influence the Government in favour of the expensive Portbury dock scheme. Yet the failure of this persuasion – confirming one very involved member of the sample in his distaste for 'politics', which, as he saw it, had ruled the decision rather than the merits of the case – and the refusal of Whitehall to grant more money for roads in the south-west, when both business and local government have over a long period jointly supported representations, suggests that the *rapport* between local economic and political notables may be often more complete than the understanding between Bristol business and the central government. The economic and social notables do not then strongly influence the local political notables through a special relationship with the centre.

Do these arguments consequently lead to the conclusion that there is no large prudential reason why men and women of this stratum need feel that they must control the leadership of the local political system, either through delegates or in their own persons? That,

Government's policy of nationalisation of dock undertakings, and the Citizens' championship of the present municipal ownership of Bristol's docks. Council Minutes, 13 June 1967, p. 58.

where the municipality rules, access is enough and leads to sufficiently satisfactory conclusions; and that, in other sectors, local government has no final power? Before deciding that this is the case it may be worth examining the possibility that there is yet another way in which municipal activity may impinge on the interests of the sample, that is, not this time their more immediate interests in their business or professional fortunes, but their interests in maintaining a particular sort of social structure, with a particular set of power relationships, in which, whether in social-class, status or élite terms, they have a superior position. American businessmen often feel closely concerned by municipal activities and take a very important part in determining their direction and content by pre-empting the field through 'civic' groups. Here, as one of the notables commented, in place of municipal affairs proper, 'the leaders of Bristol now give more time to the University, the Chamber of Commerce, the Cathedral Appeal and so forth'.[1] But is there any issue which might be construed as an attack, even if only long-term in effect, on the structure of a society which continues to sustain these notables in their leadership positions? If so, how then do they react?

Such an issue is perhaps to be found in the handling of the reorganisation of secondary education, since many, on both sides of the argument, agree that the object and consequence of comprehensive education is a tendency to greater equality in society. Comprehensive schools must be seen as a threat not only to the sort of society which on the whole wins the approval of the notables, but also to their own or their children's status-position within the society. The reorganisation of secondary

[1] According to D. C. Miller, Bristol does not look to its top Businessmen for civic leadership as much as Seattle does; *American Journal of Sociology*, LXIV 307.

education on comprehensive lines was, at the time of the interviews, and for some years before, an issue very local to Bristol, since the Labour majority on the Council had been pursuing such a policy long before the national Labour Party firmly inscribed it in its programme, and long before a Labour Government encouraged the adoption of comprehensive schemes locally. The Labour-dominated education committee had built numerous comprehensive schools in the new outlying council housing-estates after the war; then, after 1960, as this policy neared completion, the question of the future of the long-established pattern of secondary education in grammar schools in the inner suburbs and the core of the city became urgent. The political temperature gradually rose to white-heat in 1963 and 1964 when the Labour group had returned to power after a lapse of three years, and its plan for the reorganisation of secondary education in these areas, involving new relationships with the numerous well-known direct-grant schools in the city, was gestating.

Two or three declared Conservatives in the sample wholeheartedly supported Labour's secondary-school policy and one or two offset their general disapproval of it by favourable references to municipal attitudes to other educational institutions, like the University, in which they have close interests. Many were also dissatisfied with the Citizens' alternative education policy, stigmatised as too negative. However, most of the sample condemned the new Labour policy roundly as involving the loss of 'proved, established institutions' – or, as one put it, 'They're making a balls of their educational policy.'

A second very general criticism, that the programme was hastily conceived and implemented – 'the attack on education policy was rather stupidly done; it got people's backs up unnecessarily' – to some extent softened the previous condemnation since it implies that a more gradual approach might conceivably make the modification of even 'proved' institutions acceptable. Nor is there a lot of dissent from the view that post-war educational provision in the city has been very good, that the Labour councillors most directly involved in the scheme have been largely altruistic in their pursuit of their ideal, and that the administration is able. Yet comprehensivisation does represent the most fundamental divergence in policy and ideology between the two parties,[1] and there is no doubt in which direction the sympathies of the great majority of the sample lie. Besides, many are personally involved, as governors of independent, public and direct-grant schools.

What part have they played in the battle? I discovered none who has joined any of the organised groups publicly combating the implementation of the Labour scheme; the name of the chief one was included in the check-list of voluntary bodies. Many have participated as governors on deputations and at meetings with education-committee members and officials organised by a little-known *ad hoc* committee representing chairmen of governors and heads of direct-grant schools, as well as the views of parent–teacher associations. They have attempted to settle the relationship of their schools with the new public system, especially in regard to the disposition of the local-authority free places in the direct-grant schools.

The outcome of the campaign, the withdrawal by the authority of all its free places[2] at these schools, and the pushing ahead of the comprehensive scheme, lends no

[1] At local level they also differ in other important respects – for instance on land and housing policy.
[2] Restored in 1967 by the new Citizen majority.

support to the view that in a direct conflict of this sort the economic and social notables have a decisive influence in the political system. It was put succinctly by a participant in these pressure tactics: 'We had sufficient contact [with the authority], and the Press has been friendly to our point of view over the past year; our objective was not attained, not because of lack of contact, but because of our lack of political power.' Almost certainly the influence of publicly employed teachers and their representatives was greater in the formulation of the plan; in this area their degree of access and standing were greater. It can be very convincingly argued that the indirect influence of the notables on social values and behaviour is such that it is rare for working-class or Labour leaders to precipitate a conflict, but here was such a case.

The crude power of money, and the heartfelt importance of the issue to the notables were illustrated when subsequently a few very rich men, several of them included in the sample, put up the money to enable a voluntary aided school to become independent rather than enter the education-authority scheme. Consequently the decisions made or expectations entertained amongst the elected majority group (Labour) of political notables were directly thwarted. Opportunities for doing this kind of thing are perhaps limited,[1] and it must be rather rare that this resource, wealth, confined to the few, is so directly used. No doubt Citizen Party leaders are sustained in their objections to the Labour scheme by their social and political contacts with the economic and social notables but power is distributed in Bristol in a pattern which appears to conform neither to

[1] I am not aware that similar help has been extended to 'Plowden type' primary schools in the central areas where the immigrants and other deprived groups are congregated.

the model of the extreme élitists nor to that of the extreme pluralists; the unity of the notables is not absolute, nor do they dominate political decision-making, but neither is power diffused more or less equally among a wide array of conflicting narrow interest groups. What is noteworthy in the narrower context is that, although at an early stage of their interviews several asserted that they might well stand for the Council if their feelings were closely engaged on some specific issue, none has sought to join the Council on this issue of egalitarian secondary education.[1]

[1] A preference for vigorous pressure rather than for direct participation in local party politics was found in Newcastle under Lyme in some circumstances; Bealey, *et al.*, *Constituency Politics*, pp. 380–2.

# CHAPTER 8

# The Local Notables and the Local Councillors

IT now remains to bring together the scattered bits of evidence discussed in earlier chapters and to attempt to illustrate a hypothesis which will take account of the data and explain more satisfactorily the pattern of political behaviour displayed by the sample. We have seen that the relevance of local government to their main concerns, though real, is limited,[1] and partly in consequence the impulse to take leading roles in local government is limited. We have seen that where it is relevant they have easy and, if necessary, frequent access within the political and administrative systems. The otherwise mainly negative conclusions on the validity of the various hypotheses considered in the previous chapter suggest the acceptance by the economic and social notables of a pluralistic pattern of local influence, in which they concede a share of power to political notables, but which is set within a social-status system and an economic system in which influence and other rewards are distributed unequally, and to their advantage. This unequal share of influence, accessibility and benefits partly explains the willing adoption of their particular local political role.

[1] To what degree greater or less than for other groups has not been determined.

But as important an element in their reluctance to seek local representative leadership-positions is their partial alienation from the politics and the people with which are associated the final processes of civic decision-making in a large county borough today. Their pattern of participation is composed of close and frequent interaction with sections of the political system and withdrawal from other sections. The view advanced here is simply that, though very much an active part of the whole political culture, they feel estranged[1] from certain aspects of it; that the public representative arena is foreign to the kind of people from which the sample is drawn; and that this aversion helps to mould their role in the political system in certain characteristic ways. As we shall see later, in Chapter 9, the methods of recruitment and of advancement, as well as the kinds of organisation and types of relationships, are different in the institutions characteristic of the political system from those obtaining in the economic and social spheres. But the qualities of the people involved also differ, and it is these differences that will be the concern of this chapter.

The congeniality of associates to be encountered on the one hand in the Council, and on the other in business or voluntary activities is highly important to members of the sample. What matters to them is whether their associates resemble themselves in certain ways, or whether they can respect them, which is perhaps the same thing. In terms of moral qualities and worthy motivations, the notables think quite highly of a lot of councillors and candidates (Tables 31 and 34). But even this judgement is subject to significant quali-fications. There is a pervasive, even if not unanimous, feeling among respondents that political party warfare

[1] The estrangement itself being part of the political culture.

is responsible for leading councillors into intellectual dishonesty. Similarly, though the tables show general recognition of a streak of altruism in many councillors, egocentric motives are detected quite as commonly. The consensus seems to be that there is a fraction with whom service to others and to the community at large does predominate. Quite frequently, names from both sides of the Council were quoted as examples. One man described such individuals as 'some of the most outstanding men and women on both sides', and as 'really dedicated'.

But most believe that potent if not sovereign motives are, for perhaps a majority of councillors, more self-regarding. They quite commonly subscribe to the view that council service is sought after as a compensation for frustrations encountered at work or at home.[1] Two or three referred to examples of crude personal acquisitiveness in the form of real graft that had come to their notice in other, smaller authorities. Nobody suggested that anything like it ever occurred in this city, and yet the general belief that somewhere something of this sort does go on to some extent tarnishes the reputation of local government everywhere. The self-regarding motivation that was generally felt to be common and important was egotism, 'self-importance' or vanity in some guise or other – being 'in the know' and being made to feel important as a public figure, or having the opportunity to speak and to be listened to frequently and to cut a political dash; all expressed by one ex-councillor as being 'a big fish in a little pool'. It is not

[1] See Maud Report, II 9, sect. 18: 75 per cent of councillors find opportunities, otherwise lacking, to use their abilities. Sect. 19: two-thirds of manual-worker councillors, but only 13 per cent of employers and professionals, find council work more satisfying than their paid occupations. See also II 155, table 4.21 and I 139, sect. 491.

universally felt in the sample that desirable qualities can be discovered only in some social and occupational groups rather than in others; on the whole they believe that moral integrity is pretty evenly distributed among the population. Nor does any one party have a monopoly of this quality, for comparisons were by no means summed up uniformly in favour of the Citizen group; one spirited Conservative referred to the Citizen leaders as 'gutless wonders'.

When it comes to assessment of councillors' competence, their intellectual calibre, their experience of responsibility and administration, their managerial and decision-taking capacity, the verdict is sharply less favourable. One large employer says he would refuse to give a job in his business to the man who was Lord Mayor whilst he was Sheriff. Another said of 'a great friend' on the Council that he was 'well-meaning and not very clever'. A not atypical remark was 'Some seem to be quite stupid and unable to talk coherently.' Again this evaluation is particularly harsh against the Citizen group. One subscribing member of the Conservative Party who always votes Conservative in general elections finds at municipal level that many Labour candidates are better than Citizen ones, whilst another sees 'fewer real duds on the Labour side'. A third prominent party member observes with distaste, 'I lack respect for the intellectual capacity of the Citizen Party.' There is a tendency to regard Labour's leadership, especially, as more shrewd and more able. But even they are rarely regarded as good enough: 'I dislike stupid people and there have been stupid Labour men on the Downs committee.' The general, though not unanimous, approval of the competence of top officials, and the common view that they should be granted more delegated power are significant. 'Committee members

don't have big enough minds', it was said by an inveter-
ate committee woman, 'they are a burden for the chief
officers.'

All told, about two-thirds of the sample believe that
most councillors are not up to the job, and that the
Council would be improved in its capabilities if there
were included in its membership more business
managers of wide experience and of large responsibilities, and more professional people too. After all,
many present councillors are believed to be failures in
other walks of life. According to a patrician of immense
inherited wealth and high inherited position, 'a lot are
people who can't make progress in other spheres', and
this sentiment is echoed by a self-made businessman
who said, 'Eighty per cent are too lazy in their own
jobs and want to get away from work.' Invidious comparisons are made between councillors and the quality
of big businessmen, represented in the sample, who sit
on the university council, itself held up as an example of
a wise, active, decisive and resourceful body.[1] In this
rather unhappy evaluation of councillors individual
antipathies are not without their weight; one female
councillor was referred to as 'an awful woman, an
absolute tiger'. But the answers to questions about the
sacrifices entailed by their own voluntary activities, or
about the distinction between the Council and other
forms of service, give no hint of their making similar
assessments of their associates in those activities.

It cannot be supposed that prominent professional
people or businessmen would relish association on equal
terms with incompetents in an enterprise they persist in
regarding as analogous to business; and in business the
hierarchy of authority and deference is felt, at least by
those at the top, to harmonise with real differences in

[1] A view that might come as a surprise to some students and staff.

competence, experience and skill, segregating (in many social relations) the better from the less well endowed. Something like a quarter of the sample said that the poor quality of council members was a factor in their decision not to join them on the Council (Table 11). As one of them put it, 'The biggest disincentive is the mediocrity of the average member.' Non-success in business, which so many notables feel to be associated with council members, is a poor recommendation to flourishing businessmen or professional people. Business standards and ethics, with which the people represented by this sample are so thoroughly imbued, constitute a rather formidable barrier to local council work. The somewhat imperious but considerable manufacturer who would not give employment to councillors in his firm was only expressing his belief in his superiority which, if more obscure, was perceptible in the views of others.

Apart from, but reinforcing and colouring, their suspicions of the moral worth and competence of councillors, the social and economic notables are also rather conscious of a difference in social status between them and the typical councillor. Despite the bias in its representative character towards the middle class, Bristol's council, as we have seen in Chapter 7, is half-composed of people from manual working-class occupations, few are classified in the Registrar-General's top socio-economic category, and only three or four approach the social and economic eminence of many of those interviewed.

The councillor is commonly seen, and not altogether inaccurately, either as a trade unionist or as a small, not very successful tradesman. Not that the sample imagines that all or most councillors follow these avocations but they are those which seem to them characteristic of the Labour and Conservative benches respectively. Many of the sample, except some of the minority who have made their own way, are pretty clear about the contours of the social hierarchy and their position in it. We have seen above in Chapter 6 examples of the way in which informants describe themselves as 'top' people or 'patricians' and that they refer to other high-status people as desirable recruits for the Council. The identification of a large group of councillors with trade unionism is of some significance. There was a handful of notables who made rather hostile comments on trade unionist councillors, deriving from their experience with trade unionists in inferior occupational relations to them, and involved with them in conflict either on the shop floor of their enterprises, or as bargainers or would-be bargainers in front of them in the managing director's office. For economic and social notables it is not altogether uncommon to find those one refers to as 'one's work people' to be on the Council. There is a social status difference and a difference of industrial status.[1] One top manager of a big firm admitted he was influenced in his assessment of councillors by his 'reactions to union people; most of them are not very good citizens, and quite a smattering of councillors are union people, two or three from this company'. But even when the tone is not hostile it is quite commonly patronising. There was a tendency to deliver a favourable judgement of councillors in the

[1] In so large, complex and open a community as Bristol, differentiation of status must be subtle, and gradations even less crude than those in smaller, simpler, face-to-face societies; yet their role as employers perhaps gives many of these Bristol notables a more completely 'total' high status than even that of the more withdrawn rural upper classes in other areas. Cf. Williams, *Sociology of an English Village*, p. 118; Stacey, *Tradition and Change*, p. 154.

F

same tone as they say they know some 'splendid chaps' who are trade union leaders. The same inflexion of voice was present in praise of recent Labour Lord Mayors, one of whom was referred to as 'one of nature's gentlemen', whose special laudable character- istic is that 'he has no ambition'.[1]

Moreover, in view of the argument in Chapter 6, it is important to notice that, as one respondent carefully pointed out, however extensive one's contacts with the Council, committees, councillors and officials may be, they still tend not to be the kind of people the economic and social notables meet at parties and so forth. There appear to be hardly more than three men, all on the Conservative benches and all leading councillors and largish employers, who link personally and closely the local political notables with the social and economic notables. Several members of the sample mentioned one particular councillor as a personal friend or as an acquaintance or as a personal contact within the larger context of the party organisation. These distinctions receive public recognition. Included in the sample are twelve people invited to sit on the Cathedral Appeal Committee; representation from the Council was limited to the Lord Mayor and one other councillor. The appeal was looking for the distinction conferred by high, often inherited, social status, which is intimately connected with the concept of social class and is accompanied here also by the somewhat different distinction[2] of notability, both economic and social. Neither of these distinctions

---

[1] See also a letter from Sir Martin Conway to Leonard Woolf in 1922 pointing out that Woolf would have been unhappy associating with Labour M.P.s, 'though of course, among them are some delightful simple souls, very lovable', quoted in L. Woolf, *Downhill All The Way* (Hogarth Press, 1967) p. 47.

[2] To some extent earned.

is enjoyed to any degree by more than a handful of (Citizen) councillors. Besides, obituaries of defunct economic and social notables are allowed more space in the local paper than the obituaries of dead councillors; the weddings of their daughters command more attention than the weddings of councillors' daughters.

When the kinds or quality of contact subsisting between councillors and the sample are considered, we find that they tend to be very much of an official or business type. For example, while 28 of the 78 members of the sample turn out to belong to the (Conservative) Constitutional Club, only 14 of the Citizen (Conservative) council group of 51 in 1965–6 were members. While 15 of the sample are members of the more purely social Clifton Club, only 3 of the 112 members of the Council belong, all Citizens, all with some claims to social prestige other than council membership. Of the 63 members of the Merchant Venturers Society, the association of highest status in the city, 20 were included in the sample; one member of the Society is an ex-councillor; only 1 man is a member both of the Society and of the Council. The contacts between notables and local-authority people are very largely business, civic and political ones; though extensive, they lack the intensity and even warmth in forming the relationships between notables in social and business affairs, and therefore lack their salience to the notables.[1]

The notables are very well aware of these social differences dividing them from most of the Council, and well aware that the typical councillor can get rewards from council membership which are denied to a notable. Observing that none of 'the top people' go on the

[1] A gap between the local political leadership and the social leadership is noted elsewhere too; Bealey, *et al.*, *Constituency Politics*, pp. 362–5.

Council, one man added that for those people who typically do so, it means 'socially a lift-up', an elevation they can achieve neither at work nor by any other means. Another made the same point when he said, 'Many people have no status; being on the Council makes them somebody.' Indeed nearly half the sample believes that an important motive for many councillors in getting elected has been to improve their status.[1] Notables are very conscious that their own social status would not be enhanced by council membership, more likely their standing would be adversely affected.

Whatever its many faults, failures and disappointments, Bristol's formal political system possesses a considerable 'democratic' element, in that a lot of working-class people do participate in it, even though proportionately their representation on the Council is still less than that of other social classes. Not only are the notables conscious of this working-class participation, but they are also aware that it has been a largely *new* situation developing over the past 50 to 100 years, and they are also acutely aware of the concomitants of this change – the extension and deepening of the educational experience for masses of people, their awakening to social forces and circumstances, the growth of discussion, interest and participation amongst them, and the accompanying rise of the Labour Party.[2] In becoming one of the two dominant parties Labour has profoundly affected local politics, and more especially because, besides supposedly being their spokesman, it is at local level in working-class hands to

[1] Tables 31 and 32. See also Stacey, *Tradition and Change*, pp. 162, 164; Lee, *Social Leaders*, p. 41. These writers find that a considerable motive for council membership is social prestige.

[2] See Chapter 5. For the same historical process and consequences in Newcastle under Lyme, see Bealey, *et al.*, *Constituency Politics*, pp. 388, 399–408.

a much greater extent than it is nationally. It is strong in electoral terms and brings working-class people into prominence and to public notice probably more than any other social agency.[1] It brings them into relations of apparent equality with people from other social classes within the political arena and to some degree also on public occasions. Local city politics have become largely working- and lower-middle-class politics.[2] The mere change in social status of our representatives is enough in itself to have an alienating effect on the notables, but the change in social status is also translated and rationalised into a change in 'quality'. As one man put it, 'in the 1900s my predecessors were dealing with people of equal mental stature on the Council'; now, by implication, intellectual calibre has declined.

It is quite other in the voluntary bodies typically manned by the notables, and this is a considerable part of the explanation of why two-thirds of the sample feel that the satisfactions derived from local council service and other voluntary work are different (Table 18). We shall see in Chapter 9 that the patterns of recruitment and promotion to high office in these spheres are quite different. But here we must note that the membership of the Bench, of the hospital boards and committees, of trade and professional associations, of ancient charitable societies, of the Chamber of Commerce even, is congenial in that it tends to consist of people of similar

[1] Maud Report, I 137, sect. 487; Stacey, *Tradition and Change*, p. 162. The greater homogeneity of the Labour Party and the relatively similar social backgrounds of its officers and its supporters is illustrated by Mark Benney and Phyllis Geiss, 'Social Class and Politics in Greenwich', in *British Journal of Sociology*, I (1950) 316–17.

[2] Compare the withdrawal of top Yankee businessmen from Boston's politics since 1910; E. C. Banfield, *Big City Politics* (Random House, N.Y., 1965) pp. 46–7.

social, educational and often occupational background.[1]
One man described these bodies as 'the establishment',
to which he himself belongs. Another referred to the
'social *cachet*' of membership of the Merchant Venturers Society.[2] A third described in some detail the
careful processes of selection for quasi-public positions,
and observed, 'They would be nervous about having a
crank; quite a lot can be found out about people before
offering them jobs.' Several made explicit reference to
their pleasure in the company of the people they
associated with in their voluntary work, and a quarter
of the sample find satisfaction in meeting people in these
institutions, but none gave any hint that similar
satisfaction might be obtained by participants in council
affairs. Even in those rare organisations where people of
lower social status might be encountered – for example,
the British Legion – typically, respondents who are at
all active were of commissioned rank in the Forces, and
they now occupy the higher offices of the Legion in the
village or county branches. Rank-and-file membership
is left to the rank and file in non-political voluntary and
even business and professional bodies.[3]

[1] Mary Stewart, *Unpaid Public Service* (Fabian Occasional
Paper No. 3, 1964) pp. 13–17. Social organisations in other
English communities also tend to be homogeneous in class
membership; for example, Williams, *Sociology of an English
Village*, p. 121; Stacey, *Tradition and Change*, pp. 15, 81–9, 171;
Birch, *Small-Town Politics*, p. 40.

[2] The functions of organisations in lending prestige to members
is referred to by Williams (*Sociology of an English Village*, pp.
121, 126).

[3] For the reflection of the larger external status system in the
internal hierarchy of village organisations, see Williams, *Sociology
of an English Village*, pp. 121–6. See also Littlejohn, *Westrigg*,
p. 84; Stacey, *Tradition and Change*, pp. 16, 81; and Brennan,
*et al.*, *Social Change in South-West Wales*, pp. 103, 174, 175.
There is a splendid story of how, after upper-class women in a

Notables are sufficiently aware of their own status to be conscious that council membership could not possibly enhance it. In so far as it is true that a prized character-istic of council service is a rise in social and self-esteem this must have a negative rather than a positive effect on the notables, since though they are by no means averse to ego-gratification, they have reached their happy state by other, and more effective means; they are already securely recognised as community leaders, as notables.[1] The local political world can do little for their egos and their status, except perhaps to bruise and damage them.

---

Cumberland village proposed the cleaning of the local church, lower-class women scrubbed it whilst the initiators decorated the pulpit with flowers; Williams, *Sociology of an English Village*, pp. 103–4. See also Littlejohn, *Westrigg*, p. 85.

[1] See Birch, *Small-Town Politics*, pp. 115, 122, where the some-what different point is made that the weaker identification of the immigrant managers with the local community means that they prize less highly the prestige accorded by the local community and therefore seek it less. This would not be true of the Bristol sample.

CHAPTER 9

# The Local Notables and the System of Local Democratic Party Politics

'COUNCIL membership means the hurly-burly of mediocre political organisations; it is terribly wasteful, as council work is an end in itself; one would sit there having one's brain knocked about by a lot of poppycock and mediocre thought; the very nature of the activity is such as to pander to the easily satisfied, and I'm not in sympathy with a lot of the traditional amateur ways of running things.' Thus the deeply felt opinion of one active businessman, prominent in the city's cultural life. Economic and social notables see big differences between the way of life on the Council and their own, and they prefer the latter for both personal and organisational reasons.

There are crucial differences between the patterns of relationships within most voluntary and business bodies and those encountered within the Council and the political parties. The types of goals and the norms differ, therefore the organisational features differ and consequently interrelationships differ; that is, available roles and the appropriate behaviour are different in these different sectors of activity. The feature basically distinguishing between them is that the Council is characteristically a political body (though not always organised on party lines), whilst the other bodies are fundamentally apolitical (though sorts of palace politics may chequer their history).

The effects of politicisation on roles and on methods of operation are profound, and in general they are unwelcome in practice to the economic and social notables. They find competition and struggle in place of easy progress and the smooth furtherance of aims and careers; equality, even their subordination, in place of superior hierarchical position and deference; collective debate in place of individual decision-making; persuasion in place of authority; contention in place of harmony; plurality of objectives in place of singleness of purpose; cumbersomeness in place of a clear criterion of efficient operation; frustration, or at best compromise, in place of outstanding individual achievement. This chapter will outline some of the reactions of the economic and social notables to these differences as they appear in patterns of recruitment and advancement, in the organisation of Council and committees, in relations with officials, in party organisation, in political decision-making, in conflict, in the essentially egalitarian and collective presuppositions of politics, and in standards of efficiency and goal definition. These views are important to an understanding of the reasons for the limited nature of their political participation.

It will be useful to start with a comparison between the patterns of recruitment to those kinds of activity in which the notables do involve themselves, and the selection processes for council membership. Typically, selection as a member of this sort of voluntary association is not by election, certainly by no process remotely resembling a popular election to public office. As Table

F 2

11 shows, a quarter of the sample actually stated that elections were repugnant to them. Several, indeed, made the contrast explicit by underlining how much more agreeable is the process of invitation, nomination and appointment which is the normal pattern of recruitment of this sort of person to most voluntary bodies and offices, whether a highly esteemed local charitable body, a hospital board or a trade association.[1] 'Contacts', friendships, being 'known' (more particularly in quarters where selection decisions are made) are important in this process. That is why the phrase 'one thing leads to another' is so frequently adduced as an explanation for taking part in such activities. If one was little 'known' before, one gets 'known' as one accumulates the first two or three memberships or offices, and the difficulty then becomes one of refusing invitations to join more and more bodies. Squash with a local duke (to which one can come via established social status, wealth and education if one is new to the city and region) may lead to entry into a lot of positions in a variety of fields. Thus, for instance, service on the Bench is looked upon almost as a direct alternative to work on the Council. To some the choice between these alternatives appears to have been posed quite bluntly, at least in their mind's eye; a number declined both, but about 40 per cent of the sample are J.P.s. It is understood that there is some local equivalent of the Treasury's book of the 'great and the good' compiled upon local recommendations, which rules selection for the Bench and many other public and quasi-public posts (see page 74 above).

Be that as it may, the process of invitation, nomination and appointment is very much in keeping with the general conventions ruling the notables' style of life.

[1] See Mary Stewart, *Unpaid Public Service*, pp. 12–18.

They are the sought after, they rarely have to seek. The people who have the advowsons of these benefices are their relatives, friends, acquaintances, members of their own social circle, and such positions come along in the 'natural' course of events just like school, career, marriage and children: 'A lot of these things are expected of one,' it is said. As a respondent put it, 'being born into a business of a certain status and size gives one a ready-made position'; and, indeed, despite the changes in business organisation and mores of the past fifty years, some family firms still harbour the tradition which allows time to at least one member of the family to take a larger share in outside affairs. Moreover, some notables actually take over positions in charitable organisations from older relatives, illustrating once again a parallel between life at the top in Bristol and village life.[1] Some might take more positive steps to commit themselves to some such activity, but in either case no decision was required which involved a break in the accustomed way of life. Moreover, at least at the outset, the commitment seemed pretty specific and could be kept limited, and though it might speedily lead to other things for the more interested or well-connected, any one of these undertakings by itself rarely involves the expenditure of much time or study.[2]

Something analogous to this recruitment pattern is also usual in the manner of their recruitment into their business or professional careers. The importance of family connections or other social advantages in putting higher-class people on to the first steps of ladders which will take them to leading roles in industry, commerce or the professions has been well documented in other

[1] Cf. Williams, *A West Country Village*, p. 202.
[2] The magistrates' bench is an obvious exception, deep involvement in trade associations or professional bodies is another.

studies.[1] It is amongst these notables that the 'Crown Prince' avenue (42 per cent of the sample are in family firms), or the roads through somewhat more devious family or other social connections, or via higher education and managerial traineeships, are typical recruitment patterns, leading to business and professional positions of authority and influence. Such ways of embarking upon, and developing, one's career are of a piece with the method of recruitment to voluntary activities as described above.

How different all this is from the processes of selection and recruitment to representative bodies, more especially the Council, in the local political system! Owing to the hegemony of the two major parties in Bristol, which goes back to the early 1920s, there is necessarily the initial choice of party to join, and a public profession of one's choice. Then, even in the Citizen Party, there are further hurdles. After the positive affirmation of one's party colours, there will be a rather humble apprenticeship as an ordinary party member with its ward and constituency chores; competition for notice and advancement at the lowest levels; then getting selected as a candidate, and as recently as 1964 the procedure for the selection of Citizen candidates was made even more formal and 'democratic', blocking up easy loop-holes for well-connected, would-be candidates and making more difficult the success of nepotistic pressures.[2] Thereafter follows the convention of fighting one or two

[1] For example, R. K. Kelsall, *Higher Civil Servants in Britain* (Routledge & Kegan Paul, 1955); R. V. Clements, *Managers: A Study of their Careers in Industry* (Allen & Unwin, 1958); T. J. H. Bishop and R. Wilkinson, *Winchester and the Public School Élite* (Faber, 1967).

[2] For an account of candidate selection and local party electoral politics generally, see R. V. Clements, 'Bristol', in *Voting in Cities*, ed. L. J. Sharpe (Macmillan, 1967) pp. 44–71.

hopeless seats; being defeated, seeking support, entering into conflict in one's own party and with the other party; at last getting elected, only to enter upon another apprenticeship within the council group, which may well be in a minority and in no position to make policy. It used not to be like this; and today it is all quite foreign to the ways in which the vast majority of economic and social notables, of the highest or the lowest rank, have attained their status and positions.

These contrasts between the patterns of recruitment continue to differentiate subsequent developments. After joining the Council, until one attains the Valhalla of the aldermanic bench, one periodically has to submit oneself for popular re-election and to the probability at some stage of being defeated and having one's membership summarily extinguished. Re-election must follow, and advancement within the party will depend upon diligent application, on service on committees (often minor ones), on survival in all manner of controversies and on the passage of time, before entry into the senior counsels of the group is possible.[1] Moreover, some minimum amount of polite and solicitous contact with electors and supporters suffering from all manner of quirks must be maintained, and no group of councillors neglects this duty more than those from the higher socio-economic groups.[2] And all this long while the impatient councillor must wait for that party majority which, till 1967, had been vouchsafed to the Citizens in only four years since the war, before he can taste the sweets of power in making decisions and moulding policy.

Advancement in business or professional practice or even in voluntary bodies is achieved otherwise by the

---

[1] For a similar situation in Cheshire, see Lee, *Social Leaders*, pp. 171–91.    [2] Maud Report, II 110–11.

economic and social notables. On voluntary bodies they tend to be active officers, or, more rarely, inactive local branch members, or to sit on national or regional committees of such organisations. Some mentioned that, in accepting a place on some such body as a hospital board, they did so on the understanding that they would shortly become officers.

To a greater or lesser extent the journey via one of the typical pathways, earlier described, up to high business or professional position has also been easy for them. Some are so conscious of this that they confess to guilt about their limited participation in voluntary affairs, despite the fact that one criterion for membership of the sample was a fair degree of voluntary activity. A few give as a reason for taking part their sense of duty, of obligation, to repay something to the community for the agreeable way of life which in one way or another they have so largely inherited. Not merely do they tend to occupy top positions in their occupations and in the voluntary associations to which they belong, but they have encountered relatively little competition and few impediments in getting there.

But within those bodies and within the Council it is not only recruitment and advancement patterns which define the roles available to be filled and decide what behaviour is appropriate. Essentially the Council, unlike most other societies, is a political body and this characteristic heavily permeates and modifies all the behaviour, the organisation and the norms associated with it, and correspondingly fashions the roles played by the participants. Not simply, therefore, does the Council associate together people in various walks of life, of various degrees of economic and social obscurity, as we saw in the previous chapter, but the patterns of interrelations between them possess peculiar features; and many of these are antithetical to the notables.

The commitment of a local authority to the two goals of administrative efficiency and popular representative democracy creates for it problems of organisation. To achieve its ends the Council has, mistakenly or not, been organised traditionally in two different but interlocking ways at the same time. At one level, in the interests of representative debate and control it has been established as a large body organised in numerous committees, in close supervisory relations with the appointed officials. On another plane it has been organised into political parties. Both these types of organisation have been evolved in the attempt to combine full and open discussion and acceptable decisions with control of an efficient administrative system. And yet both of them, with their implications and consequences, come in for severe criticism by the notables whose reactions lie at the root of their aversion to council membership. In their presuppositions and outcomes the two types of organisation are seldom wholly separable; both are political ways of running affairs and it is this to which the notables object.

However, distinguishing between them as far as is possible, we shall consider first the criticisms of local government founded upon hostility to party politics. Many of the sample, as Tables 11 and 12 show, gave some objection to party politics as a reason for not standing for the Council and only 14 people (19 per cent) did not somewhere in their interview attack party politics.[1] According to them the solvent of party politics acts in many ways; it undermines the moral integrity of

[1] Seventy-six per cent of Conservative Party members in Newcastle under Lyme were hostile to party politics in local government; Bealey, *et al.*, *Constituency Politics*, p. 271.

the actors, it corrodes the quality of their intellectual processes, it destroys the efficiency of any organisation relying on politics for its dynamic, it is the canker consuming the essential harmony and co-operation of the group. The common failure to perceive compensating advantages or to inquire whether the true significance of these alleged drawbacks has been correctly assessed suggests some misapprehension of the nature and functions of politics.

Misgivings about the party system are occasioned by the harm it is presumed to do to 'efficiency', a standard often evoked but rarely defined by business and professional people in the sample. It is believed that damage is done by division within the Council (regarded as a sort of board of management) by irrelevant 'doctrinaire' commitment, and by attempts to win purely sectional (party) advantages. For example, according to the chairman of a very large, prosperous industrial firm, if one is used to 'business discipline and methods, one gets impatient with local government procedures, where party allegiance decides issues sometimes irrespective of the merits'. His views are echoed by many others.[1] The standard of 'efficiency' applied by the notables is evidently whole-heartedly a business one: there is little evidence to suggest that any patrician tradition has much modified it.[2] Not only that, but there is rarely any hesitation in applying it as a superior criterion by which

[1] For example, the managing director of a large store: 'So many decisions are tossed around between the two parties, they lose sight of the real thing.' A businessman with extensive interests in higher education in the city: 'It is absolutely abysmal that local politics are organised on a party basis, for a house divided against itself is inefficient.'

[2] An eminent accountant complained that municipal policy is 'too little founded on facts; fares on Bristol's buses are decided on political, not accountancy, grounds'.

to judge council affairs; if these are 'political', so much the worse for them. The view that, whatever its other virtues, 'politics' must in a general way diminish efficiency in enterprises is not uncommon outside the ranks of the notables; but for them it has peculiar significance when considering council service owing to their more than usually eager adoption of the business values which, in however vague a form, provide the standard of what 'efficiency' is, and influence their norms and behaviour.

Much of the notables' suspicion of party systems is due to their belief that corrosion of the moral fibre of the politician is almost inevitable. Politics is peculiarly 'corrupting'. It makes demands upon behaviour and inroads upon virtue apparently unknown to other activities such as business, for example.[1] While business practices may often be excused, because their functions within the wider economic system are understood and approved, political practices are forthrightly condemned, because their utility to the equilibrium of the total political system is but dimly perceived and appreciated within the notables' sub-culture. There is the crude corruption of elections for instance: 'Electoral competition is repulsive', said a highly profit-conscious financial wizard, 'as both parties promise more than they can carry out.' There is the intellectual dishonesty

[1] We saw in Chapter 2 that corrupt businessmen tend to reside exclusively in the metropolis. But see the profits made by Bristol Siddeley Engines out of contracts arranged with the Ministry of Aviation, discussed in *The Second Special Report from the Committee of Public Accounts*, Session 1966–7, House of Commons Paper 571; *The Report of the Committee of Inquiry into Certain Contracts made with Bristol Siddeley Engines Ltd*, Session 1967–8, House of Commons Paper 129; *The Third Special Report from the Committee of Public Accounts*, Session 1967–8, House of Commons Paper 192.

of speaking or voting for, or not opposing, policies with which one disagrees, and notables seem to believe this is a frequent predicament facing politicians. There is the perhaps more insidious corruption of abdicating one's freedom of will by owing a long-term allegiance to a collectivity and a set of doctrines. There is specious factionalism. Finally, another type of behaviour smelling of dishonesty is evidence of agreement, or 'collusion', as it might be called, between the parties, which arouses sour suspicions of conspiracy against the rest of the citizenry.

On the other hand, conflict of a political nature arouses particular horror amongst notables, and one facet of the corrosion of integrity by politics is, they say, the tendency of party politics needlessly to create and exacerbate divisions and animosities for quite irrelevant, unworthy reasons, and with unhappy consequences. The frequent iteration of the slogan 'the welfare of the city should come first' is suggestive of this point of view. Blinkered by prejudice, ideology, political ambition, party discipline or vain glory, councillors ignore valuable ideas and insights coming from opposing sources, reducing municipal effectiveness. Not that the notables are totally unaware that 'politics' of this sort are not confined to political institutions. One businessman, who has himself resigned from a public office to mark his disagreement with government policy, complained of the compromise, the bargaining, 'the smell of corruption', 'the political intrigue', inseparable from a local party system, but nevertheless conceded, with some bitterness, that he had encountered the same sort of thing in 'Aims of Industry'. Another admitted to meeting frustrations on a hospital board. But the head and fount of this objectionable behaviour is seen essentially as the political system. 'In voluntary work there is an intelligent

assessment of problems and solutions, there are no
vested interests,' said a cultivated professional woman,
'but in politics there is corruption and inner wheels.'

The obverse of the disputatious aspects of party
politics is the party discipline which creates a hierarchy
of authority to which members must submit their individual wills in order, if necessary by veiled coercion,
to make collective decisions. This is strongly objected
to. Like other features of the system it emphatically
colours the roles to be played. It makes an individual
contribution difficult to perceive and blurs the clarity
which is often characteristic of individual decision-
making.[1] The readiness of some notables to contribute
their specialist knowledge on specific problems, or to be
co-opted to a special committee, or to consider the
possibility of rallying to the Council in an emergency;
the attacks on the bureaucracy and delay and so forth
in the system; the general favour extended to other
voluntary activities because of the opportunity to 'make
a contribution', or to 'achieve something', or to solve a
problem[2] – all these attitudes underline the hostility to
taking part in collective decision-making in organised
democratic party politics. As it was put by the bearer
of a name long ago made a household word by his
family, 'top people are not going to tie themselves to one
party'. For democratic politics is resistant to the type
of individual leadership, responsibility, decision-taking[3]
and receipt of deference to which most of the sample are
accustomed both in their occupations and elsewhere.

Yet having noted and allowed for all the criticisms

[1] A minority of urban councillors have similar views. Maud
Report, II 129–30, 141, table 4.5.        [2] Tables 11, 14, 17, 18.
[3] Decision-making in even the most autocratic of organisations
will in fact usually be a complex matter; but the notables are not
convinced that this eliminates crucial differences between political
and other sorts of decision-making.

very generally made by economic and social notables of the working of party politics in local government, and after acknowledging its importance in diverting them from council membership, it is possible to believe that even more fundamentally important is their revulsion from democratic decision-making as such, even apart from its party aspects, though the separation can rarely be complete. That the very complex system evolved for shaping its affairs has been felt, anyway till recently, to be necessitated and justified by the commitments to popular representation and democratic control is hardly noticed. Numerous features of local council organisation and of the roles and interrelations therein deeply offend the economic and social notables.

For example, the 'quality' – largely itself a product of democratic norms – of local government as a field of endeavour, and therefore of the people who are ready to play parts in it, is often suspect. In general, representativeness is an argument in favour of large- rather than small-sized bodies, but the very fact of large numbers of councillors is itself a point of criticism for, as it was put, 'You can't have 112 able chaps.' And they cannot believe that the behaviour prescribed by the organisation can attract high-quality people. Partly because of poor personal quality, but also partly because of organisational requirements, standards of decision-making and discussion are felt to be woefully low. 'The political arena is too rough and crude, and is radically inefficient for making administrative decisions.'

Local government's complex methods of coming to decisions are quite foreign to the way in which most notables formally organise their important affairs. As well as their numbers, the large size of council committees consequent upon representational assumptions was criticised in terms redolent of a preference for a species of oligarchical or autocratic decision-making; 'the best size for a committee is three people', or even 'one person', it was said. The chairman of a large family-concern, prominent in the C.B.I., spoke of the 'frustration of delay and changes caused by committees and the maze of officialdom emasculating what one would want done'. It is felt that discussion goes on too long and that it is needlessly repeated in Council.[1] In point of fact, in so far as debate is usually curtailed in council meetings, it is a weakness, since debate in the Council is public, whilst that in committees usually is not.[2]

Relationships between councillors and officers cause some concern. There is no true parallel in business or the professions or even other voluntary bodies, of course. On balance there is a higher opinion of the upper levels of the bureaucracy than of the politicians and, though a few notables fear that consequently officials might exercise too much power, more believe that the crushing weight of disciplined party machines, the involvement of councillors in the detail of administration, the array of supervisory committees, together with the cumbersomeness and delay of the whole, unnecessarily prevent the officials operating at their full efficiency, and a good deal of sympathy is felt for them. Many notables would like to see local democracy modified to give greater scope to the officials.[3] It is

[1] Several had experienced sufficient committee work in their own voluntary activities not to be eager for more.

[2] Though many councillors are critical of the effectiveness of existing committees none in county boroughs regards them as a major source of frustration. Maud Report, II 122, 141.

[3] For example, a man closely connected with a leading city newspaper argued, 'If you can get first-rate professional people as officers you should allow them to work unfettered by committees and politics; officials always have to look over their shoulders and take into account the views of councillors,'

arguable indeed that they identify more easily with the officials than with the representatives. An almost ideal solution in the eyes of many would be an alliance between business notables and appointed officers. 'If the Council were made up of businessmen there would be a tendency to appoint first-rate officials and to leave it to them – that would be a good thing.'[1]

Yet other targets for criticism are the multifarious and often vaguely defined character of the objectives of the local authority, and the collective responsibility for them shared by all council members.[2] The doings of business and other voluntary enterprises can be seen as more detailed, more administrative and more technical even than local government's preoccupations and therefore more amenable to the business or professional man's approach to technical, limited problems. As it was put by an informant of wide business and governmental experience, 'On the Council one would have an awful feeling of frustration and waste of time, whereas in business problems are so capable of settlement, are urgent and specific.'[3]

Business or professional firms and voluntary bodies usually have a single objective, or anyway objectives that can be more reasonably grouped under one heading than the plural, and even competing, goals of local governments. To be a fully fledged councillor one has to

[1] The domination of the professionals due to the complexity of business and to specialisation noted by Lee in Cheshire has not been noticed by notables in Bristol; and would probably not be altogether welcome. Lee, *Social Leaders*, pp. 134–41, 214.

[2] A national figure, experienced in governmental committees, felt that council concerns 'are too diffuse, not intensive enough'.

[3] Compare the remark by Lord Chandos: '. . . in business you finish something . . . the work has been finished and is in being. That's the attraction of business' (quoted in Sampson, *Anatomy*, p. 548).

be in some sort a generalist, making demands upon roles and behaviour which on the whole are unwelcome to many members of the sample. They prefer singularity of aim. One notable of varied experience and responsibility in industrial politics felt he 'could contribute on only a limited front, but as an elected councillor everything comes one's way'. Because of the singleness of purpose of almost any rival sphere of activity it is argued that 'one can put more into it in a short time'.

For they feel themselves to be knowledgeable in a particular field or practised in a particular technique (even in so general an art as 'administration' or 'decision-making'). This is a reason (besides the absence of election) why the proposal for a more extended use of co-option of outsiders to help in *ad hoc* projects for limited periods receives a welcome as a method of associating them with municipal affairs.[1] Moreover, without some special means of doing this it may be difficult to see the fruition of one's own particular efforts, and the ability to do this is a very attractive feature of voluntary work elsewhere. The goals are more limited and defined; the assumption that the rational businessman's method of coming to a conclusion can be applied and all will agree is not wholly unreasonable. Many feel that the sense of achievement must be diminished if something is accomplished by political, collective means.

Yet more radical differences between the patterns of relationships within voluntary and business bodies and those within the political parties and council arouse more acute anxieties. The Council brings together people from various social strata on terms of rough

[1] Councillors also ascribe feelings of effectiveness in a committee to having a special knowledge of the subject matter. Maud Report II 119.

equality, and it does so within a framework of conflict and controversy. While, of course, conflict of some sort and degree is endemic in every organisation, and indeed in every relationship, most people shy away from conflict in the face-to-face situation; there is usually a mutual predisposition to agree, or to blur apparently opposing principles. Notables are no exception to this rule. One of the attractions of voluntary work is that 'one meets like-minded people, and friendliness and kindliness'. 'I like people to like me,' said an eminent accountant. 'I'm not a combative type.' Maintaining peace and tranquillity in interpersonal relations is relatively easily done in voluntary bodies or amongst the leadership of large firms; any debates or disputes arising there take place in an enormous sea of (at least, apparent) consensus.

It is quite different in the political arena. It is true that much of politics is about compromise, but fundamentally politics presupposes a conflict situation. And the notables are very conscious of this. Conflict in itself is repugnant to many. One man said he had 'never stood for anything', and hated the idea of doing so. Even in politics it is often remarked how politicians of different parties find themselves leagued together, and yet in politics conflict and disputation is expected, institutionalised and sometimes exaggerated. Both the trade union officials in the sample have rejected council service primarily because they have enough of conflict in their day-to-day work, partly within their own (highly political) organisations, but mainly in a perpetual round of settling industrial disputes in the district or region; yet employers in the area undoubtedly look upon both as tough, tenacious bargainers.

The notables are acutely aware of the difference between politics and the types of activity they prefer.

One put it like this, 'One can resolve conflicts more easily in voluntary work, they're not institutionalised as in politics, one can agree to differ.' An active, strong-minded woman remarked on the 'friendly and easy' relations within the societies she is associated with, contrasting them with the cost levied by political ambitions in such 'distasteful experiences as elections'. The comparative peace of these bodies is to some extent aided by the relative singleness and clarity of purpose characteristic of welfare bodies and businesses, but uncharacteristic of multi-purpose local authorities. They see themselves as 'all pulling together, but not rubber stamps'.

But beyond the objections on grounds of efficiency, lack of integrity, diffuseness and even beyond the bare facts of conflict and its institutionalisation, there is the greater stumbling-block that political conflict pre-supposes some sort of equality between the combatants, and very often criticism whose degree of radicalism a great many people rarely encounter in their normal lives. In exercising their authority, whether it be on the executive committees of welfare organisations, as incumbents of public posts, or in the boardrooms of large commercial or professional enterprises, the economic and social notables are seldom faced with a built-in opposition seeking to eject them from their positions and question-ing the validity of some at least of their fundamental premises; when dissident shareholders oppose the directors' policy it makes national headlines, there is a tremor of excitement in the business world; yet these things are common features of a party political system.[1] And to all of them one is asking the notables to expose themselves in inviting them to become members of the

[1] The irresponsible tranquillity of the board-room is noted, too, by A. Sampson (*Anatomy*, p. 478).

local Council. In their environment, part provided, part chosen, there is rarely anybody remotely or theoretically challenging their established way of life – certainly nobody to whom they would have to defer in any degree. Such a prospect on the Council deters many. For example, one managing director, very 'management-minded' and a great cultivator of human relations outside working hours, described his position in his firm as being 'the boss, to make the organisation tick as I want it to; to a degree it is a dictatorship,' he said. Discussing his own refusal to join in, 'with the Council one has always got the opposition,' said a member of an internationally known family business, 'it must be very frustrating'; for, as another remarked, 'in one's own business or in a trade association one speaks with authority, you don't have to argue'. Final testimony which may be quoted comes from a one-time Sheriff and well-known manufacturer, who said he was 'used to a position of responsibility and getting obeyed – I should be driven mad if I had to argue the toss with a lot of half-wits'.[1] What is being objected to here, by all these and other witnesses[2] is, of course, the very heart of any system of representative democracy.

This links up with the earlier point that the economic and social notables feel a councillor must find it vastly more difficult to make the kind of personal contribution for which they have such opportunities as director, partner or chairman of this or that enterprise or group. In large popular assemblies, the personal contribution of most individuals is lost in the general discussion and

[1] Notice the surprise of an ex-civil servant at the extent to which decisions are made at the top in business; Sampson, *Anatomy*, p. 548.

[2] For instance, the professional man who said, 'I don't enjoy being criticised'.

painful evolution of policy and it takes special (political) arts to get one's own ideas accepted even in modified form. Notables are well aware of this and many are revolted by it; they are appalled at the thought of trying to shift 'this vast weight' and at the small scope, as they see it, for 'individual initiative'. 'In politics you've got to put up with a compromise,' says a man of wide business interest and an active political participant in the sense outlined in Chapter 6. 'The idea is going to be mucked about, and so won't be successful.' That representative democracy is afflicted in this way is only made worse by the generally unflattering assessment of the councillors who must be persuaded and argued with, and who hold the final power of decision. After a lifetime divided between his firm and a great array of public and private positions, and membership of numerous boards and committees, an industrialist, laden with honours, still sees an essential distinction between his activity and political involvement: 'I like to get down to a job, not to listen to a lot of other people talking, especially when talking to a brief and not out of their honest convictions.' Even more vividly, one man, calling councillors 'pompous and ponderous', rather unnecessarily added he couldn't bear fools gladly, and that a Council would drive him crazy.

The logic behind the rather qualified approval of representative institutions, exhibited in Table 25 (see also Chapter 5), is now plain. Few are wholly hostile. It is most unusual to believe that voting is unimportant, but slightly more common is the opinion that 'the appointment of hospital management committees gets as good results as elections'. More sophisticated, but still rare, was the notion of an educational publisher that 'a representative system is good for supplying information and advice upwards, but it is much more efficient if it is then run like Bell Telephones'. The alternatives advocated by a small minority fit rather unhappily, if at all, within the British local government tradition. A politically active doctor argued, 'You need the kind of people you meet on the boards of the more efficient businesses; for instance, give [a member of the sample] a free hand to run Bristol and collect a team – that would be much more efficient.' An accountant, active in social work, suggested that political parties be 'scrapped' and that in their place full-time paid bodies like the boards of nationalised industries, of people seconded from the professions, be set up under a professional chairman.

Yet the limits to this aversion from the system as a system, not as a system in which one might participate, are fairly quickly drawn by most notables. So long as they do not have to take part in it the majority of the sample are sufficiently at one with general opinion to accept the costs in delay, in mistakes and in conflict, of representative democracy as preferable to the penalties exacted by many other political systems. (Some systems like anarchy do not, of course, enter their realm of thought.) The general opinion is that representative local government works less well in practice than in theory, but despite its failings no other known political system works better.[1] Rather representative of this frame of mind was a woman who, having referred to the probability that various currently neglected areas of local policy would more actively be looked into by a 'benevolent *Gauleiter*', in the next breath emphatically gave her support to representative local government, saying 'an educated democracy is what we're trying to build; an efficient boss may look all right, but is not

[1] They largely share in the consensus on basic political attitudes often noticed in this country; Rose, *Politics in England*, pp. 55–7.

desirable'. Few proposals for amendment went beyond advocacy of more delegation to officials, the reduction in size and numbers of committees, and the recruitment of top businessmen. But so great is their repugnance to direct involvement, so marked their awareness of the difference between their own and political modes of life that many concur in the view of one prominent member[1] of the sample that to go happily onto the Council, whatever marginal changes might be made, necessitates becoming almost a different kind of being.

From the notables' point of view, the satisfactions, organisation, relationships, life, roles and personnel of the political round are all so very different from those which they themselves experience and prefer that many of them regard the councillors as necessarily quite a different type, a 'political animal' *par excellence*, which they themselves are not.[2] They are very conscious of the councillors as being a special social group, with its own peculiar standards, goals and modes of behaviour. Says one, 'I do put councillors in a different category from other people.'[3] More analytically it is said that 'an extrovert will go for council work, an introvert for other sorts of work, so as not to get shot at in the market place'. Notables tend to react to councillors differently from the way they react to others, and this is not entirely explained by social-status differences. Thus one said,

[1] Since, amusingly, involved in a peculiar row in his trade, and exhibiting on national television a marked distaste for his predicament.

[2] Tables 32–4. This view is not uncommon, of course; Blondel, *Voters, Parties and Leaders*, pp. 154–5, 220–1. Blondel's discussion centres upon attitudes of big businessmen towards the parliamentary arena. In fact, the influence they exert is often a 'political' one; Rose, *Politics in England*, p. 208.

[3] A rather unkind comment of this kind: 'I feel some contempt for the councillor type'.

'I always feel a slight inhibition when talking to people I know on the Council'; and on the other hand there was an aggrieved belief that 'the two parties at the Council House join together against the traders – the outsiders'. In other words, there is more in common between politicians of opposing parties than between them and those they represent. Finally, one respondent drew a parallel with business attitudes to Westminster: 'Few big businessmen go into national politics, it is a different way of life. If you read Hansard, there is a contrast with the way in which we reach decisions – it is intolerably slow, repetitious, inefficient there. We are two different sorts of animal.'

# CHAPTER 10

# *Conclusion*

IN earlier chapters an attempt has been made to show in broad terms the position of the economic and social notables in the general social system, their part in the political system, and more especially their relations with, and their attitudes to, the personnel and institutions of the local authority. The preceding two chapters discussed various aspects of political life as lived on the Council, contrasted with the conditions and assumptions of life and behaviour in the upper ranks of business, the professions and voluntary associations. There emerged from this discussion a number of reasons for believing that the distaste so generally expressed by the sample for participation in the Council was solidly based on important differences between the social and organisational systems in the different spheres; on differences in recruitment, promotion and decision-making methods; on differences between the ideological presuppositions in forming organisations in these sectors; on differences between the kinds of people encountered there; on differences between the roles available; and on differences between the patterns of behaviour required.

The generally positive, appreciative attitudes to local government amongst the notables is in line with the sort of findings reported by Almond and Verba amongst upper-class people in this country. Instances have been noticed where some members of the sample made comments indicative of some disenchantment with representative democracy; an only half-ironic welcome to the idea of regional *Gauleiter*[1] government is an instance. Other off-the-cuff opinions about various issues are out of harmony with the radical assumptions underlying popular democracy. Comments like 'a little bit of redundancy would make people work a little harder' or 'business enterprise has built up this country' are perhaps balanced by the view that 'the unemployment of the 1930s was dreadful and an indictment of the system then'. Still, it was not an isolated opinion that 'it would be better if more time at school were spent on reading and arithmetic; the children are given more than they will ever need – there should be more vocational education'. Views on race delivered by some benign, affable, very co-operative, highly regarded community leaders are similarly inegalitarian; according to one, 'Jamaicans are bone idle and breed like rabbits; Rhodesians have only just come down from the trees; they are little above the animals, but are magnificent workers.' Another remarked on Bristol's good fortune in having so few Roman Catholics, unlike Liverpool, and so few Jews, unlike Leeds. Yet another took pride in the fact that, by reminding a trade unionist who had invited a coloured man to his home of the potential danger to his daughter, he had abruptly stopped such short-sighted though well-intentioned hospitality.

But, however startling such *aperçus* into the mental furniture belonging to some members of the sample may be, the chief impression gained from talks with the notables is one of humane conservatism. This is of a sort which seeks to preserve the essential lineaments of

[1] An expression used spontaneously by at least three members of the sample. And see comments on representative government in Chapter 7.

society as at present structured, but it is also a satisfied, relaxed conservatism; it is not reactionary, there is not a sense of their having their backs to the wall; they are neither on the offensive, nor mounting a counter-offensive. Even the views quoted above are hardly at variance with this assessment. It is not a satisfaction deriving from crude domination, but rather a satis-faction based on the knowledge, expressed or not, that the social structure, including their position within it, is almost nowhere seriously questioned.[1] Many of them are sufficiently alive to the special nature of their position that they sense a need to justify it, often by good works and so forth. What prevents any paralysis of the will like that pervading a doomed aristocracy is that they believe by and large that they *do* justify it. But their sensitivity in itself helps them to come to terms with the political system. They feel very much a part, and an important part, of the economic and social systems, and are not at all fundamentally alienated from the political system, in which they also play important though some-what more limited roles.

Indeed, despite their rejection of council membership the extent and depth of their political participation are so great that their behaviour endorses the doctrine elaborated by Almond and Verba that membership of numerous associations tends to be accompanied by greater political activity.[2] Certainly in the case of these notables greater-than-average voluntary activity is associated with greater-than-average political activity.

[1] The factors making for stability are, of course, formidable; Rose, *Politics in England*, pp. 231–3. See, nevertheless, the fore-bodings of the 'traditionalists' in and about Banbury; Stacey, *Tradition and Change*, pp. 52, 162.

[2] Confirmed elsewhere; for example, by Brennan, *et al.*, *Social Change in South-West Wales*, p. 80; and Bealey, *et al.*, *Constitu-ency Politics*, p. 200.

G

Another argument of sociologists such as Lane, Almond and Verba is that membership, even passive membership, of an organisation which is not even political in its aims is accompanied by warmer and more positive sympathy with the values of a democratic polity. Again, the appreciation of the representative system by the notables is such that this theory is certainly not disproved. If, however, it is true that certain aspects of their social behaviour lead us to expect from them both sympathy for, and activity in, the political system, and we find empirically that both expectations are borne out, why, nevertheless, is the extent of their participation quite definitely limited so as to exclude council membership? We can return to the previous analysis to find an answer to this paradox.

It will help to explain the reservations they entertain about political activity despite the wealth of their group experience if the nature of their typical roles in those groups is recalled. For we have observed that relationships within these groups are very often to be distinguished from those typical of the political system by their non-democratic features; for example, modes of recruitment and of promotion, and the correspondence between the distribution of power and position in the associations and the hierarchy of class outside them. Normally, we can assume that the individual's behaviour from situation to situation will tend to be all of a piece, that the way he plays his various roles will be more or less consistent, and, so far as possible, he will choose and reject roles, if he cannot well adapt them, in such a way that he can behave reasonably consistently.[1]

[1] Michael Banton, *Roles* (Tavistock Publications, 1965) ch. 8. Within the social system there is a tendency for each individual to enjoy either high status or low status in all his different roles, so that he enjoys something called 'total' status; Plowman, *et al.*,

It does not seem altogether fanciful to suggest that, whilst mere organisational memberships do help to tie people in a general way positively into the social and political systems, the specific roles played by individuals or groups within such associations should not be ignored when determining more exactly the connection between associational membership and political participation. The content of these social roles influences the actors' values and therefore the roles they seek to play in the political system. The specific positions of economic and social notables within their economic and social groups are governing ones and are almost wholly independent of the popular will, and may actually reinforce expectations and values imbibed as part of their particular sub-culture which are at variance with some at least of the values, like full discussion and majority voting, which are prized generally within the political system. Thus the value of democratic procedures, toleration and so forth may be learnt in their associations; but they also learn in the same associations, even to a greater degree than do others not sharing such rich associational links, the value of 'leadership', 'authority', 'high status', 'decisiveness', in their roles as officers rather than mere members of the organisations to which they belong.

These sub-cultural differences in values and normal roles can partially explain why the notables limit their political participation in such a way that they are not

---

in *Sociological Review*, x 167. Brennan, Cooney and Pollins show that this homogeneity may be unstable (*Social Change in South-West Wales*, p. 99). The example advanced by Rose hardly supports his view that individuals readily adapt behaviour to suit very different roles in different authority-systems; the different positions in which the prime minister finds himself 'go with the job' – he still speaks as prime minister of Great Britain when he deals with his colleagues in NATO. Rose, *Politics in England*, p. 119.

drawn into the realm of active face-to-face democratic discussion and persuasion, for these their other roles have not socialised them to accept. Those roles they do play in the political system have therefore rather different features from those they play in other parts of the social system, because a real dichotomy between the political and other systems is felt, and they are not altogether compatible. The apparently paradoxical behaviour of the economic and social notables in the political system is therefore designed to achieve some consistency with their behaviour in other parts of the social system, thus avoiding conflict between their roles. They redefine their political role to achieve this, as noted above, and give greater emphasis to other roles.[1]

In so far as this represents some modification of a past political role, it has been accompanied and assisted by important social and cultural changes such as the rise of the competitive managerial class, the increased emphasis on the value of business success, and the rise of the politically organised working class, which have wrought changes in their own and other people's perceptions of their roles. There are some quite strong cultural, social and often personal factors tending to influence economic and social notables towards becoming councillors or political notables, and just occasionally in individual cases these factors win and the person concerned joins the Council; but the norms of the group are usually sufficiently strong to defeat such influences, and deviants – one in particular, who was also in the sample,[2] was frequently referred to – are

[1] Recent research in 'leadership' suggests that different styles of leadership appropriate to particular social situations, and few individuals successfully adopt more than one style.

[2] In his case the norms have reasserted themselves, which explains his presence in the sample.

often treated with some derision as self-evident bad examples.

This leads to the remaining topic calling for some discussion. If it were possible to induce economic and social notables to serve in large numbers on local Councils, would it be desirable? Chapter 1 mentioned some widely accepted arguments which assume that this would be a good thing, and a quotation from an essay published in, and awarded a prize by, the *Local Government Chronicle*[1] will serve as a reminder of this view. 'Too few of the leaders of a town, leaders in the professions, business, church, trade, commerce, industry serve on local councils. These are the people who, because of their proven ability to lead, are needed on these councils, who have the task of corporate leadership.'

It can be argued that representation implies merely the guardianship of interests by elected persons. Preferable is the view that it implies also that the representatives should, through characteristics shared with the electorate, have as close an identification with the electorate as is possible; in other words, that the representative body should 'mirror' the electorate. Parliament is heavily middle class;[2] few local councils are as predominantly working class as Parliament is middle class; even Bristol's Council, shown here to be very different in social composition from most of the group of which the sample are members, is disproportionately middle and lower middle class in relation to the general population of the city. Any increase in representation of the leading professional and business figures on the Council must mean a

[1] 15 April 1967, p. 575.
[2] W. L. Guttsman, *The British Political Élite* (MacGibbon & Kee, 1963) chs 8–11; and Rose, *Politics in England*, p. 106.

diminution of working-class representation there. This reduction could be extremely severe if councils are also diminished both in number and in size. In the light of the near-hegemony enjoyed by the economic and social notables over high positions in the economic and social spheres, and their very considerable hold on all sorts of public offices, any extension of their grip into the local political sphere as well should be viewed with concern. It is a virtue, not a vice, of the English local political system that it affords opportunities for working-class people to exercise responsibility and to share power with leaders in the economic and social spheres.[1] As Mr Sharpe writes in his Tract, 'local government is the only agency which allows these [working-class] groups to make a direct contribution to the political process since Parliament like most representative assemblies is dominated by the middle class . . .'.[2] And according to Mill one of the strongest arguments for local self-government is its educative effect upon participant working men. His able middle-class administrators serve mainly to act simply as mentors to their working-class colleagues. It is indeed a merit of local government that it is not monopolised by the upper classes.

Except by the part they may take as jurymen in the administration of justice, the mass of the population have very little opportunity of sharing personally in the conduct of the general affairs of the community. . . . But in the case of local bodies, besides the function of electing, many citizens in turn have the chance of

[1] Despite W. G. Runciman's scepticism about formal machinery for participation (*Social Science and Political Theory* (C.U.P., 1963) pp. 78–86); see the 'subversive' effects of the democratic school-boards at the end of the nineteenth century; Lee, *Social Leaders*, p. 50.

[2] *Why Local Democracy*, p. 32.

being elected, and many, either by selection or by rotation, fill one or other of the numerous local executive offices. In these positions they have to act, for public interests, as well as think and speak, and the thinking cannot all be done by proxy. It may be added that these local functions . . . carry down the important political education which they are the means of conferring, to a much lower grade of society.[1]

Without their local political participation,[2] the role of the working class in our common society would be greatly the poorer, reduced to little more than to be the followers, the led, in every sphere, political as well as economic and social, wherever influence is exercised. The economic and political notables have so much, must they be given more? And whatever vices a political party staffed by professed democrats may fall into, as Michels so graphically showed and experience has confirmed, they are less likely to be fatal than the vices into which a representative political system led by people who entertain serious reservations about the norms of the system would be likely to fall. And whatever inadequacies there are in pluralist theory, experience suggests that a society in which power and position are divided in some pluralist way is more likely to survive, and even be worthier of survival, than a social system in which position and power are monopolised by a small group. Any proposed reform of local government should assist in widening, not narrowing, participation.

What now seems to be the case in Bristol is that the difficulties, obstacles and distastefulness of a local

[1] *Representative Government*, p. 365.
[2] Making possible such an 'incongruity' as a bus conductor who, as Lord Mayor, rides in a chauffeur-driven limousine; Rose, *Politics in England*, p. 76.

political career, and the attractions of competing uses of time, are now felt to a roughly equal degree by the economic and social notables, by the lower middle class and, less certainly, by the working class. So the extent of their representation depends, as with other classes, on the presence among them of people with a personal urge for political activity. That is, many of the old class advantages enjoyed by the notables – a political career as an accepted way of life, ease of entry to it at an early age, assurance of success and power – are reduced, leaving them on rather similar terms at the local level to the other social groups. They retain intimate bonds with a particular political party, and have ready access to the administration and, indeed, to the day-to-day working of the political machine. But their relations with the local political system are not homogeneous with their relations to the social and economic systems. Bristol seems to justify neither the rank pessimism of the extreme élitists nor the somewhat facile optimism of the extreme pluralists.

# Index